ON A SLEEPY SATURDAY MORNING IN LATE
DECEMBER, 1941, THE GERMAN FORCES ON
THE OCCUPIED ISLAND OF VAAGSO PREPARED
FOR BUSINESS AS USUAL...

It was still far too dark for the sentinel to see the water
two hundred feet below him. Even had he been using
his binoculars, the British submarine which was surfacing a few thousand yards to his front would have been
concealed by the darkness.

Still farther out to sea, less than a mile beyond the
submarine, a small group of blacked-out British warships escorting two former steamers sailed steadily
towards the fjord mouth. On the ships' darkened bridges
officers found themselves instinctively lowering their
voices as they approached the coastline, wondering
when the first rounds from the two nearby coastal
batteries would fall among them. How much longer
could their presence go undetected by the Germans?

The best hope of a successful operation lay in penetrating the fjord unseen, getting by that first German
lookout post before the alarm could be given. The next
few minutes would tell...

THE VAAGSO RAID

THE BANTAM WAR BOOK SERIES

This is a series of books about a world on fire.

These carefully chosen volumes cover the full dramatic sweep of World War II. Many are eyewitness accounts by the men who fought in this global conflict in which the future of the civilized world hung in balance. Fighter pilots, tank commanders and infantry commanders, among others, recount exploits of individual courage in the midst of the large-scale terrors of war. They present portraits of brave men and true stories of gallantry and cowardice in action, moving sagas of survival and tragedies of untimely death. Some of the stories are told from the enemy viewpoint to give the reader an immediate sense of the incredible life and death struggle of both sides of the battle.

Through these books we begin to discover what it was like to be there, a participant in an epic war for freedom.

Each of the books in the Bantam War Book series contains illustrations specially commissioned for each title to give the reader a deeper understanding of the roles played by the men and machines of World War II.

THE VAAGSO RAID

The Commando Attack That Changed the Course of World War II

JOSEPH H. DEVINS, JR.

BANTAM BOOKS
TORONTO · NEW YORK · LONDON · SYDNEY

THE VAAGSO RAID
*A Bantam Book / published by arrangement with
the Author*

PRINTING HISTORY
Chilton edition published in 1968
Bantam edition / June 1983

*Illustrations by Greg Beecham and Tom Beecham.
Maps by Alan and William B. McKnight.*

ISBN 0-553-23310-6

Published simultaneously in the United States and Canada

PRINTED IN THE UNITED STATES OF AMERICA

O   0 9 8 7 6 5 4 3 2 1

*To the men of three nations who lived
this page in history, and especially to
those of them who died in its unfolding*

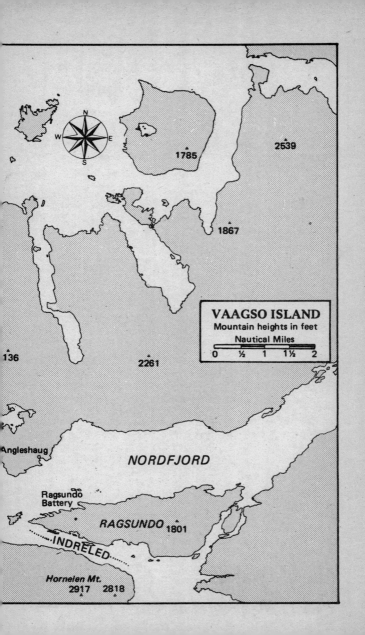

1785

2539

1867

136

2261

VAAGSO ISLAND
Mountain heights in feet
Nautical Miles
0   ½   1   1½   2

Angleshaug

NORDFJORD

Ragsundo
Battery

RAGSUNDO   1801

INDRELED

Hornelen Mt.
2917   2818

CONTENTS

INTRODUCTION

The Vaagso raid was not one of the epic operations of World War II. It was undertaken on a fairly modest scale, using limited resources to achieve a limited end, and was originally intended as nothing more than a demonstration that the offensive spirit still flourished in Britain even though the Empire had fallen on dark days.

But since earlier more tentative thrusts by British raiding parties had deliberately avoided heavily defended areas, this was to be the first real *coup-de-main* raid of the war. The objective chosen was one well worth the trouble of attacking, and the Germans counted it well worth defending. German blood would be spilled, British troops would gain valuable combat experience, and (if the raid were successful) some minor economic damage might be wrought upon the German war effort; only this and nothing more.

But in the end this small raid had consequences reaching far beyond the rocky and snow-covered mountainsides which reverberated that Saturday with the thunder of explosions and the crack and rattle of rifles and machine-guns. For the shock-wave generated by the engagement at Vaagso was to reach all the way to Berlin and ultimately into the mind of Adolf Hitler himself, who as a result of this relatively minor action would make certain major decisions destined to have a critical effect on the course of the war.

Moreover, the influence of the Vaagso raid would be felt again in the future when new operations of a similar nature were undertaken, for it was at Vaagso that a number of military innovations were first tried and proven, later to be repeated with minor modification in the legendary assaults at St. Nazaire* and

---

*For the full account of this epic commando battle, read *THE GREATEST RAID OF ALL* by C.E. Lucas Phillips, another volume in The Bantam War Book Series.

Dieppe, and finally in expanded form to become the basis for the great amphibious invasions mounted in the Mediterranean, Normandy, and all over the western Pacific.

But in December of 1941 these operations still lay hidden around the curve of the future. The fortunes of the Western Allies lay at lowest ebb as Germany consolidated her new European empire while in the Pacific Japan began building one of her own. In recent months first mainland Greece and then the isle of Crete had fallen to the Germans, the defences of Singapore had caved in, and Japanese warplanes sent the *Repulse* and the *Prince of Wales* to the bottom; the wreckage of America's Pacific fleet lay smoking amid the ruins of its base at Pearl Harbour. Amphibious warfare on any significant scale had been so long neglected as to be practically a lost art, revived briefly and bloodily during the ill-fated landings at Gallipoli and the fantastic raid on Zeebrugge during World War I, then laid away and forgotten. Armchair strategists argued that the coming of modern arms, more powerful fleets and faster and farther-ranging aircraft had made amphibious operations suicidal, as witness the horrible débâcle off the coast of Crete when a fleet of transports carrying reinforcements for the German airborne assault force already locked in combat on the island ran head-on into the Royal Navy and was destroyed with horrendous loss of life.

What little amphibious warfare doctrine existed on the allied side was theoretical, tentative and for the most part unproven, and the men who planned the brief foray against the Germans at Vaagso based their decisions in some part on past history, but in far larger measure upon their own inspiration and logical powers. Vaagso was to be the testing ground for their ideas, as well as the first real trial of a new force of amphibious assault troops whom the British chose to call Commandos.

ACKNOWLEDGEMENTS

A book such as this one does not get written without a vast amount of help from a great number of persons. I am especially indebted to the many surviving veterans of the Vaagso operation who went far beyond the limits of mere courtesy in assisting an unknown American rummaging around in their memories of what was surely one of the most important periods in their lives. Among this group I owe a very great personal debt to Admiral Sir Harold M. Burrough, K.C.B., K.B.E., D.S.O., R.N., and Major-General J. C. Haydon, C.B., D.S.O., O.B.E., the naval and military commanders respectively of the Vaagso enterprise, to Brigadier J.F. Durnford-Slater, D.S.O., and especially to Brigadier Peter Young, D.S.O., M.C., who not only put his personal papers at my disposal and answered all sorts of random questions but also reviewed a preliminary draft of most of this book and offered a great deal of invaluable advice and encouragement.

Among the many other British veterans who were particularly helpful to me I must make special mention of Colonel R. D. Q. Henriques, C.B.E.; Colonel J. M. T. F. Churchill, D.S.O., M.C.; Lieutenant-Colonel A. G. Komrower, D.S.O.; Lieutenant-Colonel D. W. V. P. O'Flaherty, D.S.O., R.A.; Major J. E. Martin, M.B.E.; Major Charles S. Head, M.C.; W.O.I. Charles C. Stacey; and Troop Sergeant-Major E. G. King. Each of these men (none of whom, unfortunately, I have ever had the opportunity to meet personally) contributed a great deal of valuable information enabling me to fill in particular gaps in the over-all picture. I am also grateful to Henry Brown, Esq., General Secretary of the Commando Association, and to the editors of the British army magazine, *The Soldier,* for helping me locate these and many other veterans of the operation. I hope that some day I may shake their hands.

I would also like to acknowledge my gratitude to Mr. Bruno

A. Schefke of the U.S. Army Language School, Monterey, California, who translated a thick file of official German war records for me, and to those imperturbable archivists of the Office of the Chief of Naval History in Washington who ferreted out the answers to several key questions in the German naval records.

The Norwegians are a reticent people and are understandably disinclined to enter into lengthy discussions of the more painful aspects of their country's part in the war, but Mr. Hans Aanestad of the Ministry of Cultural Relations and Mr. Jon Embretsen of the Norwegian Information Service in New York came to my rescue and routed out a good deal of helpful source material. When at length it seemed they had exhausted their resources Major Alf Markhus, Norwegian Air Force, happened to see my letter in *The Soldier* and very kindly wrote to me, offering his assistance. Through his good offices I received two excellent firsthand accounts of the Vaagso action published in Norwegian.

My thanks also to Robert Henriques for permission to quote some brief excerpts from his book *The Voice of the Trumpet*, and to the authors and William Kimber, publisher, for letting me take the same liberty with the books *Commando*, by Brigadier J.F. Durnford-Slater, and *Storm from the Sea*, by Brigadier Peter Young.

For other assistance in research and in locating source material, I am indebted to the following persons: Miss Laurie Jones, librarian at the U.S. Army Infantry School, Fort Benning, Georgia; Lieutenant-Colonel John Stuart McLaren, formerly the British liaison-officer at that institution; Lieutenant-Colonel Knute K. Thorpe, U.S. Army; Major Robert F. Prentiss of the U.S. Army's Magazine and Book Branch, Office of the Chief of Information; Mr. W. J. Nigh of the World War II Records Section of the National Archives of the United States; and Miss Margaret Halsted, librarian at the U.S. Army Language School.

This is far from a complete list of those who have given so generously of their time and energies to further my efforts. Without all of them, this book could never have been written, and credit for whatever success it may achieve in telling the story of the Vaagso raid must be theirs. But the manner in which I have chosen to use the material they contributed is my responsibility, and any errors, inaccuracies or wrong judgements lying within these pages are entirely my own.

J.H.D.

AUTHOR'S NOTE

Think back to one of the most exciting days you have lived through, preferably one more than twenty years past, and try to remember every word spoken at the time exactly as you uttered it or heard it uttered. You will find that it cannot be done. Chances are that a few phrases may be stamped indelibly upon your memory, but no one can reconstruct an entire conversation, verbatim, twenty years after the fact.

In order to re-create the essential flavour of the events that took place in and around Vaagso, I have found it expedient to reconstruct certain fragments of conversation and to exhume some of those chance phrases long buried in the memories of the men who fought there. In many cases documents prepared soon after the event provided an excellent starting point, and parties to the conversations quoted have searched their memories in my behalf. But I cannot guarantee that some of the lines quoted herein contain the exact words in the exact order that they were originally spoken; let it suffice to say that the approximations are as close as I and the witnesses with whom I consulted could make them.

A similar problem arose in quoting the messages flashed from one location to another as the events of that December day unfolded. Although official files bulge with other records of Operation "Archery", it is an unhappy fact that no complete copy of the Signals Log has survived to this day.

Accordingly it was necessary to reconstruct the signals quoted in these pages by using the same method discussed above. However, the format for military and naval signals is reasonably rigid, and as the time and substantive content of each of these signals is a matter of record, I feel certain that the reconstructions are fairly exact.

A more puzzling situation confronts anyone who attempts to

compare British, German and Norwegian documents pertaining to this operation. Many of the locations mentioned in these pages bear a different name in each nation's records, owing sometimes to variance in linguistic usage and sometimes to misinterpretation of which name on the map refers to which geographic feature. For instance, what the British call Vaagso is Vågsøy to the Norwegians, while the fishing community located on that island is South Vaagso to the British, Sör Vaagsöy on the map, and Måløy to the Norwegians and the Germans. The tiny island a few hundred yards from the town is Maaloy in the British records, but to the Norwegians it is Måløyna, and the Germans record it as Kulen; the Norwegians apply this last name to another piece of ground on the opposite bank of the fjord. One also occasionally encounters odd variations, such as Moldöy and Lille-Måløen.

To reduce this agglomeration of proper nouns to manageable proportions, and because the bulk of the existing records of these events are British in origin and I am essentially a lazy man, I have used the British terminology throughout the following pages.

J.H.D.

PROLOGUE

Saturday, 27th December, 1941, began on the island of Vaagso just like any other day in occupied Norway. The German sentries who had patrolled the streets of towns and villages during the last hours of the nightly curfew period returned sleepily to barracks; now at last it was their turn to lie upon their bunks and dream of home, while their more fortunate comrades who had snored peacefully through the night as the sentries crunched through the snow arose and began another day's work.

It was still pitch-dark outside as the first few citizens ventured out of their homes, for in those northern latitudes where the sun does not rise until ten o'clock and cannot peep over the neighbouring mountains until well after eleven one cannot afford to wait for daylight before beginning the day's work. There were livestock waiting impatiently in the barns and sheds, nets to be tended, boats to be caulked, shops to be opened.

The air was chilly, as it always is at that hour of a December morning, but for the first time in several days the sky was clear and stars twinkled coldly overhead. The winter gale which only yesterday had been churning up the sea a few miles away must finally have played itself out; this would be a beautiful day.

In the harbour behind the tiny island of Maaloy, in the middle of the narrow channel separating the great rocky bulk of Vaagso Island from the equally mountainous Norwegian mainland, seamen were already busy getting up steam and preparing to weigh anchor aboard three small coastal steamers; now that the weather had improved, their little convoy could venture out of harbour under protection of the armed German trawler readying itself at a nearby pier, and proceed down the net of inland waterways towards Germany.

On Maaloy itself the German soldiers who manned the tiny island's four-gun coast defence battery were sitting down to breakfast in a large room in one of the requisitioned houses they used as barracks; in a few minutes it would be time to take seats in another room to hear the monthly lecture on military courtesy presented by one of their senior noncommissioned officers. They already knew the lecture by heart, but perhaps there would be fresh news from the home front to brighten the session.

Just around the corner of the larger island, on the northern bank of the great fjord, a group of German marines left their billet in the village of Hollevik and began walking up the coastal road towards the troop mess in the nearby town of South Vaagso, the beams of their electric torches dancing on the snow. They had slept well, and the cold air felt clean and refreshing in their mouths, so they chatted and joked loudly as they strolled along.

A few miles westward, at the mouth of the great fjord, a wooden hut stood high on a rocky hillside looking out over the North Sea. The Germans used this hut as a naval lookout station, and two sentinels shared its bleak interior with a stove, a table, two chairs, a cot and a field telephone. They had passed most of the night talking about how dull a Christmas week it had been in Norway as contrasted to the excitement of the holiday season at home in Germany, but as the hours wore on and conversation palled they grew sleepy. Now one of them lay down on the cot and dozed off while the other walked outside the hut, as duty demanded he do at regular intervals, and scanned the sea below him.

The sound of the surf breaking on the shore came clearly to his ears, but it was still far too dark for the sentinel to see the water two hundred feet below him. Even had he been using his binoculars, the British submarine which surfaced a few thousand yards to his front at that moment would have been concealed by the darkness.

Still farther out to sea, less than a mile beyond the submarine, a small group of blacked-out British warships escorting two former cross-channel excursion steamers sailed steadily towards the fjord mouth. On the ships' darkened bridges officers found themselves instinctively lowering their voices as they approached the coast-line, wondering when the first rounds from the two nearby coastal batteries would fall among them. How much longer could their presence go undetected by the Germans?

Below decks in the two little passenger ships soldiers in battle-dress fingered their weapons and silently recounted their ammunition and grenades, waiting for the command that would send them up on deck to file into the landing craft hanging at the ships' davits. It had been an extremely rough crossing and many of these men had been violently seasick, but now they were in fighting trim: not particularly frightened, but tense and alert all the same. The best hope of a successful operation lay in penetrating the fjord unseen, getting by that first German lookout post before the alarm could be given. The next few minutes would tell.

This is the story of what happened when those ships steamed boldly into the entrance of Norway's storied Nordfjord and the men below decks, specially-trained raiders chosen from the ranks of the British and Free Norwegian armies, erupted into the German garrison at Vaagso. It is also the story of how their action unexpectedly changed the course of the war.

Armed German Trawler

1

SCENE OF THE RAID

The violent storms which lash the North Sea during the chill months of winter are, and have been for many generations, justly famous among seamen the world over. Like the typhoons of oriental waters they strike with little or no warning, churning the sea into a pandemonium of howling winds, stinging spray and mammoth foaming waves capable of foundering a fair-sized vessel. No seaman who has experienced one of these storms on a ship of whatever size is likely ever to forget it, and the history and culture of the countries and islands bordering the North Sea have been shaped in great measure by man's adjustment to the hazards of malign atmospheric phenomena.

Deep within the fjords and island channels which trace the rocky western coast of Norway lie a multitude of safe anchorages where even the most violent of these storms cannot penetrate. Sheltering in these calmer waters, early men built their first townsites, small seafaring villages adjoining safe anchorages nestled among the towering cliffs which plunge precipitously into the deep waters of the fjords. From these havens the Vikings sallied forth to wage war on their enemies and plunder the coasts of Britain. And as the centuries turned and the inexorable march of civilization penetrated even the wild lands of the north, the warlike nature of the townsmen and indeed of the towns themselves was gradually transmuted into a sense of kinship, of men against a harsh nature, which shaped the sense of nationalism so characteristic of modern Scandinavia. Some of the early villages grew into vast modern cities such as Bergen and Trondheim, while others are scarcely larger today than they were a thousand years ago.

In this wild and mountainous terrain the waterways provide

the principal routes of communication between cities and regions. The still fjords, some of them extending as far as one hundred miles inland, are dotted with tiny farms clinging to the steep hillsides wherever the slope of the ground allows a piece of arable terrain to be cleared. Little clusters of huts mark the remote fishing villages upon which the area's economy is so dependent. Dense pine forests spread a green blanket over the nearby mountain ranges, a soft and fragrant carpet draped carefully over the hillsides and trimmed off neatly at water's edge. Even from the fjord-side villages one may look upward during the summer and discover snow-capped peaks sparkling distantly above the forest; when winter comes—and in these latitudes it comes early and tarries long—the snowcap spreads gradually down the intervening slopes, gently covering the lush carpet of fir trees, until finally it comes to rest against the placid waters of the fjords themselves.

It is one of the most wildly beautiful areas of the known world. Small tourist steamers as well as the great cruise liners regularly traverse the area, permitting travellers from distant lands to view the natural beauties which go scarcely noticed by the native inhabitants.

Lying about half-way between Bergen and Trondheim is the Nordfjord, counted by many visitors as the most beautiful of these myriad waterways. Like a long corridor probing into the interior of the wild mountain country, its finger of salt water twists some seventy miles between granite cliffs carved out during the Ice Age. Owing to the warm Gulf Stream currents washing against its mouth, Nordfjord remains ice-free the year round; villagers who live along its shores enjoy a winter which although cold is never bitterly so, and a pleasantly cool summer. Fishing boats harboured in the fjord venture far out to sea in pursuit of the wily herring during the calmer summer months; in the winter, while storms howl over the open sea, they reap a similarly rich harvest of the many species of marine life which take shelter in the rock-oven climate of the fjords.

Close by the sea a maze of islands dots the coast of Norway. They vary in size from vast tracts of land encompassing hundreds of square miles to tiny pimplets which barely break the surface of the sea. There are literally thousands of these islands, and the network of waterways which separate them from the mainland and from one another affords what is in effect an inland channel, a passage for coastal steamers extending half the length of Norway, allowing small ships to sail serenely along in the lee of the islands while violent storms rage upon the open sea a few miles away.

Where this inner lead (or *Indreled*, as the Norwegians call it) intersects Nordfjord the waters form an inverted "T". The section of the *Indreled* which forms the stem of this "T" is known as the Ulvesund; on its left is the large kidney-shaped island of Vaagso, about eight miles long by four miles wide, and on its right the Norwegian mainland. Along the base of the inverted "T" lies the long slender island of Husevaago, centred roughly on the axis of the fjord; its western extremity fronts on the open sea at the fjord mouth and the rest of the island extends eastward four miles to a point just beyond the stem of the "T" where a narrow channel divides it from the next in a chain of islands strung down the centre of the great fjord.

At the very neck of our inverted "T", less than half a mile north of the junction of the two waterways, a steep shoulder of Vaagso Island juts out into Ulvesund. Directly opposite this shoulder one of those tiny pimple islets, some 450 by 200 yards in size, sits squarely in the middle of the channel, forcing all watercraft to negotiate the narrow passage around one or the other of its flanks. The tiny island is known as Maloyna to the Norwegians, but on maps printed in the English-speaking world it is usually identified as Maaloy; on its north shore is one of those sheltered harbours around which a fishing village has grown. The village lies snug on the lee shore of the larger island, sheltered from the winter winds by the mass of the island's mountain spine to the west and the great rocky shoulder jutting out towards the water on the south. It is known locally as South Vaagso, to distinguish it from the smaller town of North Vaagso on the northern extremity of the island facing Ulvesund.

The townspeople are a quiet and simple folk, most of them engaged either in fishing or in one of its subsidiary industries. Visitors to the town itself are few, so the citizens tend to be somewhat suspicious of strangers, but basically, like all peoples nurtured in a harsh and uncompromising geography, they are friendly: in such areas all men are forced to stand united against the common enemy, nature. They are sturdy and self-reliant, good-natured and proud, and intensely patriotic; in short, they are typical west Norwegians. They make their living from the sea, voyaging out from their sheltered harbour to net the plentiful sea fish in nearby waters, bringing them back to the small

NORTH SEA
& NORWAY

Nautical Miles

0   60   120   180

factories of the town where the catch is processed for oil and mineral products and the meat is canned for distribution to the world market.

Along the waterfront of the town a forest of piers juts out into the mirror-like waters of Ulvesund, where canneries and fish-oil plants crowd out over the water. Two large wharves provide docking facilities for coastal steamers plying the *Indreled*, and two small hotels in the centre of town and a youth hostel near its northern-edge provide comfort and hospitality to the occasional tourist. The architecture of the town is provincial Norwegian: steep sloping roofs from which the winter snow slides easily, stone sheds set into the hillside to offer shelter to farm animals, wood-frame houses interspersed with brick municipal buildings. A single road paralleling the shoreline runs the length of the town and disappears to the north, threading through a string of small settlements and villages towards North Vaagso; from this main road short alleyways and drives dart off between the buildings, dribbling away into cart-tracks extending towards the more distant structures. High in the rugged hills west of the town a dam blocks the run-off of spring thaw water down a steep gulley and the mountain lake thus formed serves as a reservoir both for the town's water taps and for the island's main power plant far below on the shore of Ulvesund.

It is a peaceful town, somewhat isolated from the events of the outside world and rather preferring to stay that way.

On 9th April, 1940, the war came home to Norway. Grey-clad soldiers of Hitler's Third Reich stormed ashore at scattered strategic points; battleship guns thundered in Oslofjord. Loyal Norwegians, united in a wave of patriotism and outrage, rose to face the invader. But it was already too late. Anger and the strength of her sons could not undo for Norway the damages caused by deceit and treachery, nor was there any way to recoup the time lost in blissfully assuming that the Germans would neither care nor dare to strike north.

As the weeks advanced and the news became worse and worse, as the smell of gunpowder hung over the length and breadth of the land, as the outclassed and outgunned Norwegian army fell back foot by bloody foot before the German onslaught, as the government fled to England and the British relief expedition was driven back out of Namsos and Narvik, the war seemed to have passed South Vaagso by. Some local citizens began to

voice the hope that, whatever happened, theirs was apparently
not a strategic area for anyone, and even the German occupation
forces might leave them alone.

This illusion was quickly shattered as the Germans settled
down to managing affairs in their conquered territory. The
strategic value of the Inner Leads had not escaped the Nazi
planners, who quickly recognized the importance of controlling
the key junctions and bottlenecks along the network of inland
channels. For although England itself had been methodically
pounded from the air the Royal Navy was still very much a force
to be reckoned with. British submarines were already making
their presence felt in the North Sea and German shipping losses
began to mount. The obvious answer was to route all possible
coastal traffic inland, along the *Indreled* whose strong tidal
currents and rugged bottom contours would exclude the British
subs; only there, under protection of the island chain could
surface vessels be entirely safe. True, they would have to venture
out into the open sea to round a few jutting mainland peninsulas
such as the Stadtlandet seven miles north of Vaagso Island, but
land-based Luftwaffe aircraft could amply protect these short
sorties which would never amount to more than a few miles of
exposed steaming at a time; after rounding the peninsulas the
coastal convoys could swing back behind the protective island
chain.

So South Vaagso found itself a garrison town, occupied by
German troops assigned to coast defence duties and control of
the inland waterways. About 240 German soldiers and 50 sailors
were stationed in and around the town, and gun positions sprouted
on the tiny island of Maaloy. The Germans established their
headquarters and a harbourmaster's office in the Hagen Hotel,
and the youth hostel became a troop billet. Norwegian families
who objected to the quartering of German officers and senior
N.C.O.s in their homes were quickly shouted into silence. Two
houses on Maaloy Island, the largest structures in that armed
redoubt, were commandeered *in toto* as barracks for the new
German coast defence battery whose guns were being installed
on the rocky ridgeline.

The Maaloy battery was armed with four captured French
12.5 cm cannons, old field guns newly mounted on improvised
ring traverses so that they could be swung through an arc of 360
degrees. An anti-aircraft gun and a searchlight were emplaced in

French 12.5 cm Cannon on ring mount

the battery's area, and two machine guns protected the shoreline in front of the heavy field-pieces.

But the battery's main defence lay across the narrow strait, at the base of the great rocky shoulder of ground south of the town. For here infantrymen of the German army began building a formidable strong point, studded with automatic weapons protected by barbed-wire entanglements. Most of these weapons were sited to fire across the front of the battery on Maaloy and thus deliver a devastating flanking fire on any raiding force so foolish as to attempt a frontal assault on the artillery position. The infantry strong point was in itself nearly assault-proof, for it lay at the top of a low cliff offering a difficult climb to any soldier able to get ashore with his back to the guns of the battery on the smaller island. The cliff fell away almost vertically into the fjord.

The battery position and its accompanying infantry protection were only a single facet of the complex of German defences which dotted the Vaagso sector of the *Indreled*. Another battery with similar infantry protection guarded the northern approach to Ulvesund from a wooded hillside near the village of Halsoer on the northern edge of North Vaagso. The Maaloy battery was itself protected by interlocking fires from a third battery situated on Rugsundo Island, four miles to the east, another in the chain

of narrow islands stretching up the middle of Nordfjord. Midway
between Vaagso and Rugsundo a naval torpedo battery was sited
at Angelshaug on the northern bank of Nordfjord to protect the
inner portion of the long channel twisting away into the mountains.
Lookout stations for the batteries were established on prominent
points of ground, one of them on the western tip of Husevaago at
the fjord mouth, where the sea approaches lay in plain view.
Armed trawlers patrolled the waterways and escorted the small
coastal convoys which traversed the area daily.

The Germans requisitioned the old garage next to the
Ulvesund Hotel and a steamer unloaded a small French tank
repainted with *Wehrmacht* crosses. It clanked noisily up the
street and vanished into the garage, whence it emerged occasionally to take part in exercises with the German infantry.

Gloomily, the inhabitants of the island—like their cousins
everywhere in the land—settled down for a long occupation,
nettled by a series of proclamations which grew more restrictive
every day. Strict blackout regulations went into effect immediately.
The Germans imposed a strict control on the movement of all
vessels, and under no circumstances was any craft permitted to
venture beyond Norwegian territorial waters; this ruling alone
had a tremendous adverse impact upon the economy of the
island, for what good is a fisherman who cannot follow the fish?

The traitor Vidkun Quisling was himself repudiated by the
Germans within weeks after the invasion. His usefulness was at
an end and when he tried to appoint himself Premier and began
issuing directives right and left most of the country contemptuously
ignored him; overnight, business came to a virtual standstill. But
the German authorities still delegated all political powers to his
Nasjonal Samling party, which became by German decree the
"state party"; all other political organs in Norway were officially
dissolved.

On Vaagso Island there were only a few members of the
Nasjonal Samling and in the end only four of these agreed to act
for the Germans, the others either disclaiming their former party
affiliation or at least assuming an obstinately passive role. It is
worth noting in the light of present world conditions that not all
members of the *N.S.* in prewar Norway were traitors at heart;
some proved to be sincere patriots who had simply been duped.

The possession of private radio transmitters was forbidden,
upon pain of death. The Germans took over the only public
transmitter in the town for their own purposes, principally that of

jamming British broadcasts to the Continent. It was forbidden to listen to any broadcast from an "enemy" country in a public place, which included hotels and boarding houses. In one's own home, one might listen to programmes from other countries abroad so long as no news broadcasts were included; news broadcasts from neutral Sweden in particular were anathema in the eyes of the occupation authorities.

The playing of the Norwegian national anthem was strictly regulated, permissible only upon prior written approval by the German authorities; later, as relations between the populace and the occupying power deteriorated, it was banned completely. Citizens might display the Norwegian flag "without restriction"; however, demonstrative flying of flags on the birthday of the exiled King Haakon (who, to the German way of thinking, had ceased to exist) was prohibited. Proclamations and edicts of the former government and the government-in-exile were banned from circulation and publication.

The noose grew ever tighter. The Germans published a lengthy list of proscribed books. Mere possession of any of the books on the list, which included a number of pre-war bestsellers, became a criminal offence.

Citizens were summoned to turn in all firearms to the German authorities; henceforth possession of a weapon would be punishable by death.

In South Vaagso the canneries and fish-oil factories were urged to continue normal production, but now there was a difference in the marketing: most of the products of the factories went direct to Germany in bulk shipments. Most of the factory owners co-operated unwillingly and only under duress, but one major factory was owned by an *N.S.* member who did his best to comply from the very start.

Tension continued to build up in Norway. A predicted German swoop on the country's few Jews soon followed, and they and even their distant cousins with one-quarter Jewish blood were rounded up and shipped off to concentration camps in Poland. Other religions came under fire, and fought back; the *N.S.* party got into a full-scale battle with the clergy. In the autumn of 1940 Norway's seven bishops banded together as the "Christian Council for Joint Deliberation". The following winter they published a scathing pastoral letter concerning German interference with religious freedom, and the Germans banned the letter from circulation. But the spirit of resistance was beginning to flower: citizens made copies of the bishops' letter and passed them on to their friends, and in the form of a chain letter it got as wide a circulation as it might have enjoyed if the Germans had permitted publication.

And then the sabotage began. On a late November night in 1940 serious landslides occurred throughout western Norway. Curiously, they all took place at exactly the same hour but at widely separated points. Rain and snow had loosened the topsoil to such a degree that only very small charges of explosives were needed to put it in motion. The damage was extensive. Massive slides put the Oslo-Bergen railway out of service for a full week, blocking the line at ten separate locations. A highway cut into the cliffside along Hardanger fjord was completely wiped out. It was obvious what had happened, but the Germans were never able to prove anything. Their only recourse was to a series of mass arrests, which of course only served to aggravate the tension even further. The sabotage went on.

The population at large scorned those few citizens who collaborated openly with the enemy, but there was not really very much they could do about it. The newly-formed underground dealt very effectively with a few of the worst offenders, but this only led to more reprisals against innocent persons. For the most part all the citizenry could do was ostracize the collaborators socially. Boycotts against pro-German businessmen were strictly forbidden, and to be caught trying to organize one meant deportation at best. And any attempt at violence against their persons occasioned harsh reprisals.

So passive resistance became the watchword in Norway, just as it was in many another occupied country. Citizens made a point of ignoring the Germans, of looking right through them, and to the average citizen a collaborator was just another German. They began to go out of their way to ignore the enemies of their country; it became a fine art, for the practitioner had always to avoid stepping across that fine line where he could be held accountable for his words or actions as an act of "treason".

The Norwegian soon learned that one of the most potent weapons in his arsenal was his highly-developed sense of humour. A German soldier walked into a department store in Oslo one day, gave a very correct fascist salute to the lady behind the information desk, and said:

"*Heil* Hitler! Can you direct me to the lingerie section?"

The lady looked up in some amusement, and without batting an eye clapped her right hand to her heart.

"God save King Haakon! Two floors up!"

The cryptic legend I₇I (a symbolic abbreviation for King Haakon VII) and the meaningful number 1918 (a year the Germans would have liked to forget) began to appear chalked on walls, and *Leve Kongen!* (Long Live the King!) proved easy to write in the snow with a pointed stick. The humourless Germans soon announced that anyone on whose property these patriotic *graffiti* appeared would be liable to severe punishment. Within days the phrases began appearing only on the property of known collaborators.

The islanders of Vaagso too were growing restive. The German occupation troops, doing their best to act correctly towards the civil population while enforcing what they considered reasonable enough orders, met with a frosty and over-formal courtesy, well calculated to stop short of anything that might be counted insolence by an overheated Prussian, infuriating more for the finer points of courtesy neglected than for those observed.

A story went the rounds to the effect that a boy fishing from a pier in Bergen had watched a German soldier on a bicycle, his attention distracted by a pretty blonde going by in the opposite direction, take a wrong turn and ride off the pier into the water. When the soaked and infuriated soldier gave him a dressing-down for not having called out a warning, the lad was contrite and respectful: "I feel terrible about this, sergeant. It was all my fault. But you see, I had been listening to Radio Berlin and thought you were bound for England."

But others sought a more useful gesture than simply chaffing the conquerors. In Vaagso, as was happening elsewhere in Norway, a few young men began to disappear. Sometimes they sailed out in their fishing smacks and never returned, and sometimes they simply vanished from their beds at night. Months later a smuggled message from Oslo might notify a particular relative or friend that young Edvard had safely reached England, where the government-in-exile had its seat and a new Free Norwegian army was being organized.

The Germans trumpeted their military successes of 1940 and 1941 to a politely disinterested Norway, while the people hardened in their hatred towards the oppressor and in their resolve to be rid of him. Incidents took place and blood was spilled on both sides, but the spirit of resistance continued to grow. In a report submitted to Berlin late in November of 1941 the German Army of Norway stated wearily that "the mass of the population is in sharp opposition to Germany". Oddly enough, the Germans seemed puzzled by this inhospitable attitude.

The population of Norway was indeed in sharp opposition to Germany. The people had never lost their faith that the end of the war would ultimately bring the complete defeat of Germany and the liberation of their country. The citizens of Vaagso made the same private prayers each Sunday as did their countrymen throughout the land.

And although they could not possibly know it at the time, a rude surprise for the particular Germans walking among them was already under preparation in London.

2

SPECIAL SERVICE BRIGADE

When the events of 1940 forced Great Britain to fall back into a strategical defensive role, Prime Minister Winston Churchill was among the first to recognize and state the requirement for continuing to conduct at least small-scale offensive actions. The evacuation of Dunkirk had barely been completed and talk on the streets still centred on the possibility of a German invasion of England itself when Mr. Churchill, in one of the memoranda he was fond of firing off to Cabinet Ministers, Chiefs of Defence Staff, allied governments and anyone else whom he wished to prod into taking some immediate action or decision, wrote:

> . . . But if it is so easy for the Germans to invade us, in spite of sea power, some may feel inclined to ask the question, why should it be thought impossible for us to do anything of the same kind to them? The completely defensive habit of mind which has ruined the French must not be allowed to ruin all our initiative.

It is of the highest consequence to keep the largest numbers of German forces all along the coasts of the countries they have conquered, and we should immediately set to work to organize raiding forces on these coasts where the populations are friendly.

Only two days later, on 6th June, 1940, the Prime Minister issued another memorandum to the Chiefs of Staff enlarging on his concept of coastal raids:

> We have got to get out of our minds the idea that the Channel ports and all the country between them are enemy territory. . . . Enterprises must be prepared, with specially-trained troops of the hunter class, who can develop a reign of terror down these coasts, first of all on the "butcher and bolt" policy; but later on, or perhaps as soon as we are organized, we could surprise Calais or Boulogne, kill and capture the hun garrison, and hold the place until all the preparations to reduce it by siege or heavy storm have been made, and then away. The passive resistance war, in which we have acquitted ourselves so well, must come to an end.

It was as a direct result of these two memoranda that the War Office came to organize the Special Service Brigade. The brigade was placed under the personal control of the hero of Gallipoli and Zeebrugge, Admiral of the Fleet Sir Roger Keyes, who was designated Director of Combined Operations, or simply D.C.O. in the jargon of the War Office. As the originator, organizer and prime mover of the classic Zeebrugge raid of 1918, Sir Roger was the obvious choice to set new enterprises afoot; forceful in his manner and caustic in his speech, he need take a back seat to no one in knowledge of the unique demands of the type of operation the Prime Minister envisioned. In a peculiar way they were two men out of the same mould: visionary, courageous and determined; merciless with fools and blunderers and contemptuous of those who would procrastinate when the hour cried for action. But somehow the incisive rhetoric of the parliamentarian was more persuasive than the pungency of the sailor and Keyes would always manage to make as many official enemies as he did friends.

The new Special Service Brigade was a loosely affiliated

grouping of battalion-sized elements formed entirely from soldier volunteers on detached service from their parent units. These elements, and eventually the soldiers in them, were designated "Commandos", adopting an old Portuguese word in vogue during the Boer War as a title for small bodies of troops detached for raids and other special missions. There were to be twelve of these commandos in the brigade; each would contain a small headquarters element plus ten raiding troops of three officers and forty-seven other ranks each, and would be capable of completely independent operations.

Under the stewardship of Admiral Keyes the commandos soon began a cautious exploration of their own potential. The first operation, a small "pin-prick" raid on the French coast only a few weeks after Dunkirk, proved nothing except that even if troops got ashore successfully they could accomplish little of value without a great deal of specialized training and careful planning.

In mid-July of 1940 a larger force attempted a raid on Guernsey in the Channel Islands. The aim was to secure information of the German garrison, bring back a few prisoners, and to raise as much of a row as possible in order to upset the Germans' digestion. An incredible succession of mishaps and blunders ensued. Untrained R.N.V.R. boat crews had to cruise around in the dark for hours looking for the right beach. At last the troops got ashore but then were unable to find the German garrison, which was not in its supposed cantonment. A rapidly-rising sea made a mess of the re-embarkment, and the raiding force barely got away, having had to abandon part of its equipment. All in all, the operation lacked polish. Good men had risked their lives to bring off the raid but, owing to faulty planning and inaccurate intelligence of the target, had come away with nothing to show for their effort.

The chaotic aspects of the foray against Guernsey were duly noted by the Prime Minister, who appended just one icy footnote to the after-action report: "Let there be no more Guernseys."

The lessons of the Guernsey operation were apparent enough, and throughout the remainder of 1940 and into 1941 the brigade stepped up the pace of training. Nothing less than perfection would do from here on. The pace was relentless, but standards of proficiency soared, and men soon found themselves doing things they had never dreamed they could do. When a unit commander proudly reported that his men had marched twenty miles in three hours carrying full kit he was told to teach them to march twice that distance in less than half the time. They became expert poachers, learning to move through the forest as silently as Red Indians. Two scarred Shanghai police inspectors gave lessons in knife-fighting and the most effective killing techniques for an unarmed man to use against an armed opponent.

Standards soared; muscles hardened. And as combative instincts sharpened and the soldier developed new sets of conditioned reflexes his confidence grew and he began to crave action, *real* action, against an armed enemy.

At last the welcome news came: another raid was being planned. The objective this time was the Lofoten Islands off the northern tip of Norway, and this time nothing went seriously wrong.

The only problem was that the landing was virtually unopposed. The Royal Navy played its part to perfection, and the ground troops were trained to a new high both in personal and in team competence. The whole raiding force was spoiling for a fight, but after gathering in the twenty-man garrison and about two hundred unresisting German merchant seamen the British could only blow up a few factories, collect all the German documents at hand and depart unscathed, accompanied by a swarm of eager Norwegian volunteers.

By this time several complete commandos of the brigade were fully manned, equipped and trained, and they were eager to sink their teeth into a more satisfying chunk of the German army. In succeeding months a number of promising plans were set in motion but to the immense disappointment of the waiting troops these were invariably cancelled at the last minute, sometimes after the raiding parties were already embarked and at least once when they were in sight of their target. At each new cancellation Roger Keyes screamed like a wounded eagle, but all he accomplished was to alienate a few more of his supporters in the higher councils of the nation; his influence was clearly on the wane.

No one who has not himself seen military service can fully appreciate the adverse effect a cancelled operation has on troop morale. It would seem that the soldier should be immensely relieved that he need not go out to face death or mutilation on schedule, but if preparation for the operation has brought him to the correct psychological peak the opposite will more likely pertain. Mankind has come a long way from the days of dwelling in caves and fighting with clubs and stone axes. Killing and facing the corresponding risk of being killed is no longer a natural condition of our daily life, so a good wartime training programme must build up the soldier's confidence in his personal invulnerability in much the same way that a football player convinces himself that so long as he tackles hard and clean any bones that break will be his opponent's. The more this programme succeeds in building up the soldier's fighting spirit just prior to his entry into action, the greater the frustration he feels if that action fails to materialize—and the more difficult it will be to reach so high a peak the next time. That the offensive spirit of the commandos was able to survive so many letdowns and still burn brightly when action came is not the least of history's many testimonials to the calibre of the men themselves.

By October of 1941 Roger Keyes had succeeded in making enemies of so many people in high places that no enterprise under his sponsorship could ever expect full co-operation from all the various agencies upon whose support its success would depend. Reluctantly, the Prime Minister acceded to the growing demands for the testy old warrior's removal and released Keyes into retirement.

Mr. Churchill's choice of a successor for the old sea dog came as a surprise to all the services, for he appointed a relatively junior officer to this important post. Captain the Lord Louis Mountbatten, Royal Navy, had distinguished himself in the Mediterranean theatre of operations, where one of his more notable accomplishments had been sailing a ship that was to all appearances already sunk—the destroyer, H.M.S. *Kelly*, riddled by German fire, torpedo-holed and riding so low in the water that most of her main deck was awash—safely into harbour against improbable odds. When she was patched up and pumped dry he took her out again, winning new honours before she was completely shot out from under him, after which he and his crew underwent the harrowing experience of being machine-gunned in the water while swimming for their lifeboats. He had a flair for handling men, combining quick intelligence and cavalier daring with an air of personal charm that gave him the very persuasive powers Roger Keyes so unfortunately lacked.

Upon arriving at his new headquarters Mountbatten announced his intention to conduct at least one raid per fortnight. These raids might be relatively small affairs such as infiltrating a handful of men in rubber boats to knock out a coastal radar station, or they might involve the landing of battalion-sized forces escorted by destroyers or even larger warships. What was important was that the Germans should be continuously tormented. Accordingly, a target committee set to work, scanning maps of the enemy coastline and combing intelligence files, searching out suitable targets for commando operations, evaluating their relative worth and vulnerabilities and assigning target priorities.

Based upon experience gained from the first tentative operations, a fairly rigid set of rules for selecting targets for combined operations was soon established and set forth in a memorandum at Combined Operations Headquarters:

(1) Select a sector of the enemy coast about which there is adequate information relative to the enemy defences.

(2) Of the portions of this sector on which it is possible to land, choose the one which may be most easily approached without detection.

(3) List all possible targets within this portion which lie within a mile of the sea. Eliminate those which are either too strongly defended to offer a good chance of success or too weakly defended to be worth the trouble of attacking.

(4) Of those remaining, select the ones which:
   (*a*) Are convenient to good landing places;
   (*b*) Can easily be found by the landing force;
   (*c*) Are just outside of enemy concentration areas.

(5) All other things being equal, pick the target nearest to the sea.

During the month of October the target committee, guided by these principles, compiled a list of possibly remunerative objectives scattered from the northernmost tip of Norway to the French-Spanish border. The Royal Air Force representatives in Combined Operations Headquarters laid on missions to get up-to-date photo coverage of each of the chosen areas.

And so it was that on 29th October, 1941, a twin-engined bomber with the distinctive R.A.F. roundels on its wings skimmed up the *Indreled,* passing briefly over Vaagso two times before it disappeared beyond the steep hills bordering the fjord, with a spattering of fire from the German anti-aircraft gunners on Maaloy speeding it on its way.

3

"ANKLET-ARCHERY" PLAN

The Ministry of Economic Warfare had early seized upon the Norwegian fish-oil industry as a worthwhile target. There were two reasons for its surprising strategic importance.

The first was that fish oil is particularly rich in glycerine which in time of war is always a valuable commodity, being one of the basic ingredients in the manufacture of military explosives. The German war machine had not failed to exploit this most productive source, and tons of the valuable stuff were shipped off monthly to the munitions factories.

The second reason was less obvious to the military mind, but any mother of young children could have pointed it out in a flash. Fish oil is a particularly rich source of vitamins A and D, the so-called "sunshine" vitamins. It happened that the *Wehrmacht* had a critical need for continuing stocks of these nutrients, especially for the submarine crewmen plying the Atlantic convoy routes whose duties in the enclosed steel cocoons of their ships—coupled with the outright hazards of surfacing during daylight hours—denied them any exposure to direct sunlight for weeks at a time.

The fish factories in the Lofoten Islands usually account for about half the industry's total production in Norway, so Operation "Claymore", the almost unopposed British raid in March of 1941, had been a severe blow. At one stroke the main factories at Stamsund, Henningsvaer, Svolvaer and Brettesnes were blasted out of action; repairs and reconstruction began immediately but would take a great deal of time. The Ministry now turned its attention to the secondary seats of the industry, and for the first time the name of Vaagso began to appear in intelligence folders in Whitehall. Under the prompting of the Ministry its sub-agency responsible for clandestine operations on the continent, Strategic

Operations Executive (S.O.E.), considered the possibility of knocking out the fish-oil factories in South Vaagso through acts of sabotage. After a careful comparison of the available intelligence data and its own resources S.O.E. declined the job, arguing that the risks were too great; the cost to the local population in terms of probable German reprisals against outright acts of sabotage could not be justified by the degree of damage saboteurs might inflict on the factories.

The problem was now turned over to the combined operations planning staff at Richmond Terrace. Could they perhaps do something about the factories at Vaagso?

It happened that at the time the staff was considering a return visit to the Lofotens. Repairs on the demolished factories were coming along nicely and before things progressed too far it might be a good idea to provide more discouragement for the Germans. A few visionary souls suggested putting a force ashore there to establish a permanent base for operations against German shipping at Narvik and along the northern coast, but the problem of air cover obviated anything so ambitious. German bombers could pound such a force to pieces at their leisure, as the Lofotens were far beyond the range of British aircraft in even the northernmost bases; even a short-term landing would require some type of diversionary action to tie up those Luftwaffe elements within striking range of the islands.

Under the criteria for target selection which we have already examined Vaagso looked like a first-rate target for a combined operation, accessible from the sea and defended by just enough German troops to make the job challenging without making it downright suicidal. The Royal Navy enthusiastically endorsed the idea on the premise that a raid within the normally safe inner leads might scare coastal traffic out into the open where it could be more effectively dealt with by British submarines.

Accordingly the staff drafted a new plan, outlining a two-pronged operation against the Lofotens in the north and Vaagso in the south; both attacks would be launched simultaneously. The northern effort was tentatively given the code name "Anklet" while the prospective thrust against Vaagso was labelled "Archery".

This plan was still in outline form when Lord Louis Mountbatten succeeded Roger Keyes as Chief of Combined Operations. At his first briefing on current projects the "Anklet-Archery" plan caught his eye and his interest. After reviewing the concept of the operation and considering the forces available to mount the two attacks he gave his approval for detailed planning to begin immediately.

The wheels were set in motion and further intelligence on the prospective targets began coming in from a variety of sources. Force commanders had to be selected and forces earmarked. Mountbatten wanted the northern and southern force commanders each to work out his own detailed plan while the C.C.O. staff co-ordinated the two efforts and gave all possible assistance to the designated planning teams. All the facilities and resources of C.O.H.Q. would be placed at the disposal of the two force commanders.

It was the custom at C.O.H.Q. to designate an over-all commander for each major operation, normally the head of the major command from whose resources most of the operational forces would be drawn. Mountbatten was fond of referring to them as "our patrons". The combined "Anklet-Archery" effort would require a great deal of naval activity and as the fleet elements required could best be made available by the Home Fleet its Commander-in-Chief, Admiral Sir John Tovey, K.C.B., K.B.E., D.S.O., was designated "patron" of the operation and given over-all responsibility not only for supervising the whole operation but also for keeping German naval elements currently in northern waters off the backs of the two assault forces.

On 6th December the commanders of these forces were named.

In the north where the German garrison was still negligible in size the task would be primarily a naval one, with a commando force carried along principally to do the demolition work and to deal with any Germans not bright enough to throw in the towel when they saw British warships closing on their position. So a naval commander was appointed: Rear Admiral L. H. K. Hamilton, D.S.O. The elements under his command for the "Anklet" operation would hereafter be known as "Force J", and would include assorted ground forces drawn principally from Number 12 Commando, under Lieutenant-Colonel M. S. Harrison, M.C.

But in the south no one service would predominate. Originally the "Archery" half of the plan was envisioned as a diversion, to harass the enemy coastal defences and draw attention away from the more vulnerable force in the north. To accomplish this aim the Royal Navy would have to penetrate the inner leads by night, a problem calculated to grey the hair of the most confident sea warrior; then a commando force would have to fight its way ashore, overcome a sizeable German garrison occupying prepared defence positions, and perform its own destructive tasks; meanwhile the Royal Air Force, operating at extreme range, would not only have to keep the Luftwaffe off the vulnerable ships channelled in the restricted waters of the fjords but also keep it so occupied that no German aircraft could be diverted northward to engage the unprotected "Force J". The R.A.F. would operate from home stations on a fixed timetable, but both naval and military elements could be expected to meet with any number of contingencies and ought to have senior commanders on the spot. This seemed the one situation where the classic principle of unity of command ought to be violated, and Mountbatten and Tovey chose two joint commanders for the "Archery" operation, taking care to delineate the specific responsibility and authority of each. They were correct in doing so, for one does not violate established military axioms lightly, but they need not have concerned themselves with the potential problems of inter-service rivalry or overlapping authority in this case. The two men chosen, strangers to one another until 6th December, complemented one another's personalities so perfectly that from the start they worked in complete harmony, like two skilled musicians getting together for a duet.

Rear-Admiral Harold M. Burrough, C.B., R.N., was a gunnery specialist of wide repute and possibly the least excitable senior officer in the Royal Navy, a service long noted for its aplomb. His most recent combat action had been the escort of Convoy PQ–3 over the hazardous northern route to Russia, and despite the tensions of the voyage no one could afterwards recall having heard him raise his voice.

An Oxford graduate who later trained in H.M.S. *Britannia,* Harold Burrough had first been blooded during World War I, serving as gunnery officer of a light cruiser during the Battle of Jutland. In the years between the wars he undertook a series of assignments of ever-increasing responsibility, until the outbreak of the second great war found him manning a desk as Assistant Chief of Naval Staff at the Admiralty as a newly-promoted rear-admiral. Chafing at his desk as his contemporaries sailed off to battle, he sought and won sea duty again, getting himself posted as Flag Officer Commanding, 10th Cruiser Squadron.

The news of his appointment as naval commander of Operation "Archery" came as a surprise, for he had never had anything to do with combined operations beyond paper exercises while attending various staff courses. The challenge was a welcome one.

The choice of a military commander was delegated to Brigadier J. C. Haydon, D.S.O., whose Special Service Brigade would have to provide the troops for the operation. The tentative plan called for one full commando backed up by small elements of several others to make the landing, and at first glance the obvious solution seemed to be to name the lieutenant-colonel commanding the main element. But the subordinate elements of the landing force would be quite scattered, and the military commander ought logically to remain at the command post aboard the flagship where he would have ready communication with all of them. Haydon knew that none of his lieutenant-colonels would sit still for this; every one of them, if asked, would insist upon his prerogative of going ashore at the head of his troops, and ought rightly to be there. After brief reflection he informed Mountbatten that he would prefer to serve as military commander himself. The nomination was accepted immediately.

A regular officer of the Irish Guards, Charles Haydon had twice distinguished himself in delicate assignments before being appointed to command of the new brigade. As military assistant to Leslie Hore-Belisha when that stalwart war secretary was setting forth various useful reforms of the military establishment during pre-war years, he demonstrated a combination of energy and tact notable even in the halls of parliament. In May of 1940 he won admission to the Distinguished Service Order for his part in a dangerous special mission to the Hook of Holland to arrange the escape of the Dutch royal family and key members of the Netherlands government. He was more persuasive than authoritarian, the sort of leader who makes his personality felt in the ranks without being obtrusive but still gets his way and produces the desired result in rapid order. As Brigade Commander he gave his junior officers a relatively free hand in developing their units while he watched from above, keeping channels open, encouraging, standardizing those ideas that seemed particularly good and quietly discouraging those which were obviously over-ambitious, soothing the fire-eaters who burned with impatience to take on operations beyond their early capabilities.

He was almost fanatically devoted to the principle of thorough and detailed advance planning for tactical operations, which he insisted was the surest way to minimize casualties; it was, in fact, to his adherence to this principle that the commandos owed much of the credit for their success in operations where the risks seemed at first glance prohibitive.

Military planning, like politics, is really the art of the possible; in these terms one might define the purpose of the commandos as widening the realm of the possible.

The choice of a military commander had been relatively easy, but the choice of assault elements from among the twelve commandos of his brigade was a difficult one for Charles Haydon to make. Each of them was eager to get into action, and each commanding officer felt that his own particular commando was obviously superior to the rest. One full commando and a few elements of another would be employed at Vaagso, but approached from the opposite direction this seemed merely a choice of which ten commandos to disappoint by default. The brigadier spent some time in meditation, comparing the relative strengths, experience and state of training of the twelve.

In the end he selected Number 3 Commando, under Lieutenant-Colonel J. G. Durnford-Slater, to do the job and Number 2 Commando, which was then off on a training course in the Scottish highlands, to provide the major supporting elements.

4

NUMBER 3 COMMANDO FORMED

The first circular letter that went out from the War Office to units in the field requesting volunteers for "special service" was rather a vague document in that it gave no indication of the nature of the services for which the volunteers would be liable. It did specifically state that the men would not be required to perform parachute jumps (unless they later offered to do so) and promised that each volunteer would be privately interviewed by an officer who would give him some idea of what was involved and a chance to withdraw his application. As general guidelines the War Office suggested that interested personnel should not consider volunteering unless they were good swimmers, immune to seasickness, physically fit, above average in intelligence, self-reliant, and possessed strong initiative.

This unusual document was received with considerable interest at a certain Royal Artillery training depot. The first man whose desk it crossed, in the normal way of all military correspondence, was the adjutant, a Woolwich-trained captain with a receding hairline, a deceptively mild manner of speaking, and a rather bland air about him which sometimes put new acquaintances in mind of a harried bank clerk.

The son of an officer killed in France during World War I, John Durnford-Slater had served many years in India, a period he looked upon as the happiest of his military career. Now at the age of thirty he chafed at the relative inactivity of his assignment to duty behind a desk in England, shuffling papers for hours on end and accompanying his commander on troop inspections while the future of the empire hung in the balance and enterprises of critical importance were being set afoot elsewhere. Training recruits was important work, but it was not satisfying.

Viewed from this perspective, the letter before him was irresistibly attractive; above all, it seemed to hold promise of the one thing he craved above all else—action. He read it through a second time, thought for a few minutes about what he was going to say, and then hurried into the colonel's office. "Look at this, sir," he remarked. "The War Office wants some of our people for special duties of some kind. If it's all right with you, I'd like to put my own name at the head of the list."

The colonel was not at all disposed to let a good adjutant go, but after a brief argument Durnford-Slater's earnestness prevailed and the older man gave in. When Durnford-Slater pointed out that he would need a letter of recommendation, the older man smiled. "You've been a soldier a long time, John," he said. "You go ahead and write it yourself and I'll sign it."

Captain Durnford-Slater returned to his desk and drafted a glowing description of his own soldierly qualities, got it signed and posted it off. The interview which took place a few days later was notable chiefly for its obscurity. Durnford-Slater learned only in the most general terms what he had volunteered for, but he left his name on the list.

The incident was soon forgotten. Weeks passed, and the daily paperwork showed no sign of abating. Durnford-Slater's impatience with garrison life grew ever greater, though he was too much the regular soldier to voice his complaints. Then one day he entered the colonel's office on a routine matter and found his superior studying a piece of paper. Looking up, he eyed his adjutant speculatively for a moment. "I say, John," he said cheerfully, "I should have read that recommendation of yours more carefully before I signed it. It must have been a real work of art. Have a look at this signal that just come in from the War Office."

Curious, Durnford-Slater took the proffered document and glanced through it quickly; shocked, he read through it a second time, much more carefully:

CAPTAIN J. F. DURNFORD-SLATER ADJUTANT 23RD MEDIUM AND HEAVY TRAINING REGT. R.A. IS APPOINTED TO RAISE AND COMMAND NUMBER 3 COMMANDO IN THE RANK OF LIEUT-COLONEL. GIVE EVERY ASSISTANCE AND RELEASE FROM PRESENT APPOINTMENT FORTHWITH AS OPERATIONAL ROLE IMMINENT.

In something of a daze he took leave of the replacement depot and caught the first available train up to London, where he reported to the War Office for instructions. Here he received a brief orientation on the structure and purpose of his new unit and was directed to get it recruited, organized and operational in a very great hurry.

He also found out that he had already achieved a singular distinction. From the initial list of volunteers a handful of promising young officers had been carefully selected, promoted as appropriate, and designated to command the new units. As Numbers 1 and 2 Commandos had not yet been organized (they were meant to be recruited later from the Royal Marines), Number 3 was the first of the commandos to be activated and Durnford-Slater was the first commando soldier of the war.

But there was no time for reflection now; too much had to be done. An entire battalion-sized unit had to be recruited, organized and trained from a standing start. Durnford-Slater had by now learnt what the mission of his new unit was to be—raids upon the enemy coast—but he had little idea just how one went about doing that sort of thing. It did not much resemble anything he had ever done in the Royal Regiment of Artillery, except possibly pig-sticking during his off-duty hours in India. Better to worry about the exact tactics later, he decided, and concentrate on picking some good subordinates right now; at least he did know something about sizing up the candidates for a job. He took the list of officer volunteers he had been provided with at the War Office and, armed with a rail warrant, set out on a round of interviews to select the best-qualified officers for his troop commanders and staff.

One of the first volunteers he interviewed was Second-Lieutenant Peter Young of the Bedfordshire and Hertfordshire Regiment, who later recorded his impressions. Ordered to an appointment at Romsey, he made a wild trip on a motorbike through foul weather.

"By the time I reached Romsey I was in a desperate mood and ready to volunteer for anything, particularly if it did not involve motor-bicycles. I was an hour later. The interviewing officer, happily, was two hours late.

"Eventually I was ushered into the presence of a captain who bore, I thought, a superficial resemblance to Mr. Pickwick and certainly looked benevolent. This, I said to myself, will be some staff officer from the War Office. He asked me in a quiet voice whether I was 'all for this sort of thing'. His precise meaning was obscure. I stared at my questioner with the look I imagined people used in the wide-open spaces and said 'yes'. He asked next if I knew anything about small boats; much experience of canoeing on the River Isis justified me in assuring him that my knowledge was extensive. I was in."

It was nearly two weeks before Second-Lieutenant Young learned that the mild-looking captain he met at Romsey was the commanding officer of his new unit, and had somehow risen in a fortnight from captain to lieutenant-colonel!

Within those two weeks, quite a lot took place. Durnford-Slater selected his troop commanders and staff; the troop commanders in turn took the same list and went out and chose their own subalterns. Then each troop's three officers took the "other ranks" volunteer list in hand and set about recruiting their men. It was not always an easy task. The men themselves were willing enough, but their present commanders were loth to let them go; after all, the type of soldier described in the War Office circular is just the type any commander will fight to retain. Ingenious obstacles were thrown in the way of the commando recruiters by stubborn battalion and regimental commanders. But Durnford-Slater had chosen officers with initiative and anyway the whole project had Mr. Churchill's personal seal of approval so in the end the interviewers had their way. In an incredibly short time Number 3 Commando was up to strength and a waiting list had been established to fill any vacancies which might occur.

The Special Service Brigade was unique in the British Army. Each of the twelve commandos was for all practical purposes an independent unit with its own depot in some obscure small town. Headquarters space was requisitioned by the government but there were no barracks: every commando soldier received a small subsistence allowance over and above his regular pay with which to provide himself with food and lodging somewhere in the vicinity of his troop headquarters. He made his own arrangements with his landlady and was responsible for impressing upon her that she should keep his comings and goings to herself, even if he disappeared without any notice for weeks at a time. He trained hard, and he expected to fight hard; in return for this, he had his off-duty hours to himself, living in a private home with his free time (what there was of it), his to spend as he pleased, with no barracks inspections or bedchecks. It was a privilege viewed by the rest of the army with considerable jealousy, but the commando soldier earned it many times over. The standards he was required to meet in other matters were almost fanatically high.

John Durnford-Slater kept a number of firm goals in mind while he whipped his new unit into shape. The first and foremost of these, as Peter Young recorded, was that Number 3 Commando should be the Greatest Unit of All Time. The second was that it should be the first of all the commandos in the brigade to see action. He had his own ideas about discipline and incentives, and these became policy from the start.

Discipline was rarely a problem. In that the commandos were designated and treated as élite units there were always more volunteers available than there were vacancies to put them in. The men were handpicked by their officers, who were usually shrewd enough to spot potential troublemakers in advance. But despite the most careful screening an occasional misfit found his way into the unit, and Durnford-Slater found it expedient to be ruthless in dealing with these men. The first time a member of Number 3 Commando stepped out of line he found himself standing at a rigid and quivering position of attention in front of his colonel, who tore great strips off him in a few painful minutes of mostly one-sided discussion. If the offence were minor, the miscreant was then returned to his duties, with a stern warning that the next transgression would bring the ultimate punishment, for there were no courts-martial in the commandos.

This ultimate punishment, from which their was no appeal, was known by the dreaded acrostic R.T.U.: returned to unit. The commando soldier always remained a member of his parent regiment, being carried on its rolls as "detached for service" with the commandos. It took only a simple one-sentence request from Durnford-Slater or the commander of any of the other commandos to send a man back to his regiment, and he banished from the commandos forever. No explanations were sought, and no excuses accepted. R.T.U. had the finality of broken glass; it could never be undone. It was also a way out for the soldier who found he did not like commando duty: he had only to ask the colonel once and he was returned to his permanent unit without prejudice to his record.

The best incentive Durnford-Slater could offer any man for exceeding the already-high standards of Number 3 Commando was promotion, and he used it skilfully in encouraging initiative and leadership. Once the ranks were solid and all vacancies filled, he ruled that newcomers must enter at the lowest level. This meant that no future replacement would be admitted to the organization except as a second-lieutenant if he be an officer, or as a private if an "other rank". Sergeant Smith of the Guards was more than welcome to apply for service with Number 3 Commando provided he agreed to enter as a private and compete with all other ranks of the commando for promotion. In a surprising number of cases, Sergeant Smith was more than willing to accept these terms. What with R.T.U.s and operational losses there were frequent vacancies for promotion in the commandos, and a really good N.C.O.s chevrons had a way of finding their way back to his sleeves before a great many months had passed.

"The system of making all officers joining Number 3 Commando start their service in the rank of subaltern," observed Durnford-Slater years afterward, "sometimes caused us to miss star turns, such as Lord Lovat,[1] but in other ways had much to recommend it. All officers serving in the Commando knew that

---

[1]Captain the Lord Lovat declined service as a second-lieutenant in Number 3 Commando, and eventually found a captaincy in Number 4 Commando. Within a year he rose to the rank of lieutenant-colonel, and commanded the unit during the D–Day assault on Normandy. Like Durnford-Slater and Young, he was a brigadier by war's end.

they would not have new officers coming in to take up the captain's vacancies. It was up to all our officers to compete for these vacancies and the best man won.''

Durnford-Slater had seen his second great aim—that Number 3 Commando should be first to see action—carried out when his unit was selected for the attack on Guernsey during the summer of 1940. The unit was hardly well-trained at that time, but the ensuing farce played out on and around the island was principally caused by faulty intelligence and poorly-trained R.N.V.R. boat crews. It did point up a few deficiencies in the commando's training, though, and by the time Number 3 Commando was chosen to participate in the Lofotens landing in March of the next year the deficiencies had been made good. Durnford-Slater led his men ashore in the best fighting trim imaginable, but there were few Germans about and none of them was inclined to fight. So Number 3 Commando went home still spoiling for action; the blow had fallen on air.

Soon afterwards the commando underwent one of those periodic convulsions which every soldier learns to dread: reorganization. High military headquarters have a disconcerting habit of announcing from time to time that it is necessary for their subordinate units to reorganize, which is a euphemistic way of announcing that the subordinate units must rip themselves to shreds and rebuild from scratch along entirely different lines. Sometimes this process serves no purpose other than giving an illusion of progress while standing still, and sometimes it really does achieve some finite gain. The problem is that the soldier in the subordinate unit never knows in advance which is going to be the case, and he enters the process with serious misgivings. For a mercifully brief period confusion reigns supreme; lights burn late and tempers grow short. No one is quite sure just where he fits into the new structure, nor what channels now exist for getting things done. Gradually order begins to emerge from the chaos, but the growing pains which had probably just about ended in the previous arrangement go on for a long time.

In this instance each commando of the brigade was directed to reduce the number of its subordinate troops from ten to six. By way of compensation, the surviving troops each gained fifteen men, and the commando headquarters gained considerably. It meant a net loss in the commando's fighting strength and might have forced some R.T.U.s except that the actual effective strengths were low at the time anyway. For example, the largest

Higgins Craft (ALC)

troop in Number 3 Commando numbered only about forty men at
the time, so the problem was principally one of reshuffling
personnel. One of the aims of the whole process was to bring
each troop's authorized strength—now three officers and sixty-
two other ranks—to almost exactly the load capacity of two of
the new Higgins landing craft that were beginning to arrive from
America. In the end, it turned out to be a good thing: the
colonels found six troops much easier to manage than ten, once
the dust had settled, and they really did not lose anyone except
on paper.

As the initial planning for a raid on Vaagso began in
Richmond Terrace Number 3 Commando was at its base at Largs
in Scotland, running through a cycle of training exercises to keep
the edge on some of its still-untested skills. Located on the Firth
of Clyde, Largs is a pleasant holiday resort for the city of
Glasgow, and it made an ideal site for a commando unit in
training. The unit had moved north early in 1941 and took to the
place immediately. The Victoria Hotel became headquarters for
Number 3 Commando, while other hotels and boarding houses
scattered throughout the area provided ample billeting space for
all hands. Behind the town was a huge uninhabited area of
mountain slopes and rocky crags, perfect for staging all sorts of
training schemes, including a number where live ammunition
was sprayed rather liberally about the landscape. The hills were
unforested, mostly bleak moorland with deep tussocks of gorse
and heather; it was very hard country for marching. The profu-
sion of rocky coves and small sandy beaches along the coast
afforded excellent sites for practice landings.

By this time the unit was pretty well shaken down. The
obvious misfits had long since been R.T.U.'d, everyone was fit

and trim and knew his job, and morale was high. A projected landing on Pantelleria proved to be only another false start, but everyone was still feeling confident and more than a little cocky. There was time to fit a good bit of athletics into the training schedule, and everyone from the commander down took part; Durnford-Slater was a bear on physical fitness. To the regular soldiers long accustomed to service in regiments commanded by fifty-year-old colonels it was always startling to see their young commander churning wildly down the middle of the football field, his knees working like pistons and tacklers rebounding in all directions. There was also a liberal leave policy in effect, much more liberal actually than the one authorized by the brigade commander. Durnford-Slater sometimes made a practice of releasing the whole unit for a day or week-end, less one troop who would be detailed to bustle about purposefully among the buildings of Largs, smartly turned out at all times and ready to salute like mad if the brigadier happened to drive through. This deception was eminently successful; on at least one occasion when 2 Troop, the smallest of the six troops, had the duty, Brigadier Haydon took the trouble to call Durnford-Slater after passing through and compliment him on the particularly smart appearance of the whole commando.

In that most of the members of Number 3 Commando knew each other pretty well by now, it might be a good idea if we got acquainted with at least the key men, for it is their separate characters and personalities which we shall see shaping the events at Vaagso in the pages to come.

Number 3 Commando's new second-in-command, Major J. M. T. F. Churchill, M.C., of the Manchester Regiment, was one of those splendid military eccentrics upon whose presence in its ranks the British Army so rightfully prides itself. "Mad Jack" Churchill won his Military Cross during the campaign of Dunkirk, which city he had finally reached puffing and sweating along on a bicycle, the longbow with which he had sworn to bag himself a German slung across the handlebars. He would not consider going into battle without his sword, a broad-hilted claymore harking from those same highlands which inspired his dubious skill at playing airs on the bagpipe. In combat he was courageous to a fault, inventive and entirely unpredictable. Later in the war, before his bold misadventures inevitably landed him in a German prison camp, he would win admission to the Distinguished Service Order by capturing over thirty Germans in a single night, stalking them individually and in pairs in the darkness, then leaping out of the shadows with a cry of *"Hande hoch!"* while brandishing his sword wildly over their heads.

Durnford-Slater's closest army friend, Lieutenant C. S. "Charley" Head, had been quick to follow his old chum into Number 3 Commando, where he now served officially as Signals Officer and unofficially as Durnford-Slater's right-hand man. The two had met late in the 1930s when Durnford-Slater was assigned to a camp in the south of England and had been partners in a great number of light-hearted adventures; years afterwards they shuddered to recall how many times they might have faced court-martial. Charley Head was a tall Cornishman who had at one time planned to become a veterinary surgeon but found soldiering even more to his liking; one of those people to whom leadership just comes naturally, he was a military jack-of-all-trades and probably the most widely-feared "scrounger" in the Southern Command when he came to the commando.

The balance of Durnford-Slater's personal staff consisted of Captain Alan Smallman, the adjutant, a dark-haired regular soldier from the R.A.S.C.; Captain (Doctor) S. D. Corry, a sturdy and courageous Irishman who served as the commando's medical officer; and the administrative officer, an elderly and distinguished-looking captain named W. E. Martin but known to his associates as "Slinger".

"Slinger" Martin handled all "Q" duties in the headquarters of the commando and supervised the same functions—equipment, clothing, ammunition, pay, billeting—in each of its six troops. To the performance of these duties he brought a richly-varied background of military experience. His military service had begun during World War I when he served as a trooper with the 9th Lancers, but shortly after the war he transferred to another regiment where before long he rose to the post of Regimental Sergeant-Major, and later Quartermaster. He held a number of army-wide championships in horsemanship and shooting, and as an administrator had no peer. His pragmatic approach to unusual problems was well illustrated by the way he managed to make himself available for transfer to Number 3 Commando: he simply went to the nearest medical officer and got himself declared too old to accompany his regiment to the Middle East. But he never felt too old to demand an active role when the commando had an operation going, and before the war ended he saw more combat than most younger soldiers ever did.

Working under the control of this variegated headquarters were six troops that were almost as diversified in character as was the staff, each troop tending to assume the personality of its commander to a considerable degree. Captain Bill Bradley, a tall and rather wild northern Irishman, led 1 Troop, and though the troop was not composed exclusively of his countrymen it sometimes seemed to be. Lieutenant Bob Clement of 2 Troop was a temperamental Scotsman, completely at home in the climate of Largs, possibly a little inexperienced when it came to infantry tactics but with plenty of dash and ginger.

Captain John Giles of 3 Troop was an outstanding athlete—among other distinctions he held the heavyweight boxing championship in Southern Command—and one of those rare people who seem able to do anything well. His men held him in such awe that it almost bordered on worship, for he had an automatic sense of command, apparently limitless physical endurance, was approachable and interested in their problems, and could invariably outdo them at anything they tried. One hot summer afternoon he brought the troop in from a long cross-country march in full kit. Placing himself at the head of the column, he ordered "column left" as they passed the main pier and without further word marched the whole column off the end of the pier. As he bobbed to the surface at the head of his men he calmly ordered "column right" and in perfect formation the troop swam back to shore and marched away under the gaze of dozens of astonished onlookers. The men of 3 Troop would follow their captain anywhere, without question.

4 Troop's Captain "Algy" Forrester sported a bristling moustache which contrasted oddly with his otherwise dapper appearance. He was the firmest disciplinarian among the troop commanders; "a real Prussian" in the words of one of his subordinates. He had been a newspaper correspondent by profession but when war came he trained as a gunner. As such he entered the commandos without the faintest idea of infantry tactics, but compensated for this by a driving determination to "get on with the job" and a willingness to learn. His great love was mountain-climbing, a hobby which permitted him to make an invaluable contribution to Number 3 Commando and ultimately to the whole brigade.

One night, after the commando had spent a weary day

splashing in and out of small craft in simulated beach assaults, he and his junior subaltern, an Australian lad named Bill Lloyd, showed up at Durnford-Slater's door with a proposition.

"Look, Colonel," began Forrester, "this landing on the obvious beaches is a mug's game. The Germans will always be waiting for us with machine guns. Bill and I have worked out a technique whereby we land at the most difficult places. Nobody will be expecting us there and with the right kind of training we could get ashore unopposed."

"What sort of places do you have in mind?" Durnford-Slater asked.

"Oh, cliffs, rocks, almost any place would be better than flat beaches. If the Germans have got machine guns on the shore a low cliff could provide some kind of deadspace to cover us during those critical seconds when we're all bunched together piling out of the boats. Look, there's nothing to going up a cliff if you know how. Let me train a few people in the technique. If it works out we can train a lot more. Maybe everybody."

The idea appealed immensely to the colonel. It might be well worth the trouble, and even if it did not work out, the training and experimentation would help break the monotony of road marches and target shooting.

Under Forrester's direction 4 Troop first did some practice landings in rocky coves, then at the base of low cliffs, and finally at the foot of the steepest drops the Scottish coast could offer. Before long they had it down to a drill: the boats grounded, one or two "ace climbers" scaled the cliffs with ropes, then everyone swarmed up the ropes. In a short time Lloyd had qualified as an "ace climber", and then he and Forrester trained others, first from 4 Troop and then from the rest of the commando. Soon everyone was scrambling up and down sheer drops like a herd of goats, and the other commandos of the brigade began sending cadres for training. When the King paid Number 3 Commando a visit Forrester's men put on a demonstration for him; soon the cliff-climbing activity became so closely identified with the commandos that the two images remain linked to this day.

And, as Durnford-Slater reflected, it was a wonderful thing for morale. A man who can climb a sheer cliff gets the feeling that he can do anything.

5 and 6 Troops were the "work-horse" elements of the commando, being commanded by the two officers with the broadest background in infantry tactics and drilled accordingly. 5

Troop's Captain A. S. "Sandy" Ronald was the senior troop commander in Number 3 Commando; 6 Troop was commanded by Peter Young, who had by this time risen to captain himself under Durnford-Slater's competitive promotion system.

Despite being still in his middle twenties, the Oxford-trained Young was counted an "old pro" by his fellow troop commanders because he had seen action during the Dunkirk campaign, from which he returned as liaison officer to Brigadier Barker of the 4th Division. Until Dunkirk, Young, like so many young professsional soldiers awestruck by the *Wehrmacht*'s brilliant string of blitzkrieg conquests, had considered the Germans an unusually terrifying foe; but during that brief campaign he made a significant discovery—"if you shoot them they bleed" —that changed his whole outlook on the war. Now he was working to impress that same message on every man under his command, at the same time making sure that they learned everything he could teach them about infantry tactics.

The high morale of the whole commando was a tribute to Durnford-Slater's philosophies of leadership. Neither a series of administrative reorganizations within the Special Service Brigade, with all their resultant frustrations, nor a string of cancelled operations could do much to Number 3 Commando's *esprit*.

Part of the key to this success lay in variety. Durnford-Slater liked to change the type of training frequently to prevent the men from going stale, varying the pace, preferring to build to periodic peaks and slack off occasionally rather than trying to be a hundred per cent in everything a hundred per cent of the time, which is generally a losing game. Everyone was encouraged to come up with new ideas for unusual training schemes to break the pattern; Jack Churchill and Peter Young proved to be especially inventive in this respect. Young even managed to give the colonel some useful experience of infantry tactics, frequently inviting him down to 6 Troop to "observe" a new exercise and then at the end of the orders group announcing: "The colonel will command the second movement group".

Nonetheless, as the autumn of 1941 began to give way to winter there were signs that some of the fine edge was wearing away. Little things during the day hinted at a growing sense of weary futility among the men: what was the good of all this special training if they never got to use it? Surely there must be some Germans somewhere they could try on for size?

The officers were just as restless as the men. They even

worked up a plot to infiltrate a few men into Ireland and blow up the German embassy in Dublin, which Doctor Corry and Bill Bradley were sure was aiding the U-boat campaign by relaying information to Berlin concerning convoy movements. Much to his own surprise Durnford-Slater gave his blessing to this absolutely unauthorized venture. Charley Head was rounding up explosives with Corporal King of 5 Troop and Doctor Corry was departing for Dublin on leave to reconnoitre the objective when Durnford-Slater received an urgent telephone call: he was to recall all members of the unit presently on leave and to report himself to Combined Operations Headquarters in London the next morning to discuss a new operation. Although he did not know it yet, the target this time was to be Vaagso, and this time the operation would *not* be cancelled.

5

"KOMPANI LINGE"

The ninth day of April, 1940, will probably stand forever as the blackest day in the history of Norway. The nation was caught unprepared by the carefully-planned Nazi onslaught, and by nightfall her fate was sealed. Scattered units of the Norwegian army fought on for two full months, but the issue was for all practical purposes already decided.

Martin Linge, a popular young character actor, was appearing with the national theatre company when the national mobilization order cast him in a new role: he reported forthwith for active duty as a lieutenant in the army reserve. Assigned to a unit near his Andalsnes home, he fought with distinction through the dark days that followed, until a splinter from a German stick grenade ripped into his foot while his company fought in support of the British landing at Romsdal. Hustled aboard a hospital ship amidst a group of British casualties, Linge soon found himself in England.

While he lay convalescing in a British hospital, the chiefs of S.O.E. happened to start casting about for someone suitable to

German Stick Grenade

head a proposed Norwegian section. A Norwegian-born surgeon on the hospital staff heard about the project and mentioned Linge's name as a likely prospect; an interview was soon arranged. He made a strong impression upon the mysterious gentlemen from Baker Street, who liked his poise and took note of his quick intelligence and visible hatred of the Germans. After a memorable audience with the exiled king, who commissioned him a captain in the Free Norwegian Forces, he was named to head the new unit, designated the 1st Norwegian Independent Company.

We have already seen how during the early years of the war numbers of young men began to disappear from Norway, only to reappear weeks or months later in England. They represented a fair cross-section of Norwegian manhood: mechanics, farmers, lawyers, fishermen, artists, shopkeepers. There was only one common denominator beyond their nationality, and that was that every one of them was driven by such an intense loathing for the Germans that he had risked his life to reach England where he might prepare to take an active part in ejecting them from his homeland.

Upon arriving in England and being screened and interrogated by British authorities to ensure that no German "plants" were among their number the newcomers were put in touch with their

government-in-exile. Those who appeared particularly well suited for military service of a strenuous and unusual nature were
passed on to Martin Linge for vetting and, if found suitable,
seconded to his new command.

S.O.E. had made a wise choice in asking for Linge's
services. His stage training gave him the poise to deal with
personages of whatever rank and station. He had an exceptionally quick mind, a personaltiy that invited confidence, and was
adept at making rapid and accurate assessments of strangers. A
slender but well-built man with somewhat aquiline features, he
exercised command in the informal and casual manner which
came most naturally to him, but in combat he was capable of
acts of impetuous courage. As will any military unit commanded
by a leader of strong personality, the company soon came to
reflect Linge's character as a kind of composite personality of its
own. Inevitably, it came to be known among the Norwegians not
as the 1st Norwegian Independent Company but simply as
Kompani Linge.

Headquarters in London was established at Kingston House,
formerly the Norwegian Embassy and now the seat of the exiled
government. Even a quartermaster section and storehouse was
somehow squeezed into a corner of the basement, so that in the
end the company became a truly independent and self-sufficient
military unit, sponsored and manned by the Norwegian government-
in-exile but supplied by and under operational control of S.O.E.
Later in the war it would provide the nucleus of specially-trained
saboteurs and intelligence agents to be infiltrated back into
Norway, landing from fishing vessels on moonless nights or
parachuting into the bleak vastness of the *Hardanger Vidda,* but
the initial training in 1940 and 1941 was directed along roughly
the same lines as that received by the British Special Service
Brigade. It became, in fact, a company of Norwegian commandos.

Under such circumstances it was only logical that *Kompani
Linge* should become more or less an unofficial adjunct to the
Special Service Brigade, even though nominally they operated
under the control of two entirely separate sub-branches of the
Ministry of Economic Warfare. It became normal practice for the
brigade, when contemplating an action in Norwegian territory, to
ask S.O.E. to make all or part of the company available to
participate; this not only gave the operation a joint flavour and
provided interpreters to handle any necessary dealings with the

locals, but also in a surprisingly large number of cases turned up men with an intimate knowledge of the objective area.

During the Lofotens raid in March elements of the company had gone ashore with 3 Commando, and Durnford-Slater and Linge met and had a chance to size one another up; each liked what he found and a warm feeling of mutual respect and admiration grew between the two men.

Now, as the detailed planning for the "Archery" and "Anklet" operations began to gather momentum, S.O.E. once more agreed to put elements of *Kompani Linge* at the disposal of each of the landing force commanders.

6

OPERATION "ARCHERY"

The proposed operation against Vaagso began to take shape long before Durnford-Slater was called to London from Largs. Military, naval and air representatives had long since put their heads together and come up with a rough plan for the operation. When Mountbatten approved their outline plan they immediately began filling in the details.

The initial concept of the operation called for all of Number 3 Commando, supported by one troop of Number 2 and augmented by specialist detachments as needed, to land during the last minutes of full darkness and accomplish a number of tasks: they were to destroy the German battery on Maaloy, kill as many Germans as possible in the general area, demolish the main fish factories and wharves as well as the German-operated radio station, seize whatever enemy documents, codes and instructions came to hand, arrest known collaborators, and then withdraw. If this seemed a large order, the planners felt that surprise and split-second timing could bring it off. The Royal Navy would carry the troops to the objective, deal with whatever German naval elements might be in the vicinity, and sink merchant ships hauling supplies for the Germans. The Royal Air Force would

H.M.S. *Onslow*

maintain a continuous fighter umbrella over Ulvesund to ward off
German air attacks and draw the attention of the Luftwaffe away
from the more vulnerable "Anklet" force to the north.

The expanded plan generated considerable enthusiasm at the
Admiralty, and the requisite warships were selected with a great
deal of care. H.M.S. *Kenya,* one of the new and speedy Fiji-
class cruisers mounting twelve six-inch guns, was chosen as
principal fire-support vessel and would serve as flagship for the
expedition. Three of the newest, fastest and heaviest-armed
destroyers in the fleet, H.M.S. *Onslow, Oribi* and *Offa,* would
back up *Kenya* with their own four-inch guns, and the slower but
even heavier-armed Hunt-class destroyer H.M.S. *Chiddingfold*
would use its four four-inch anti-aircraft guns to deal with any
German aircraft that might slip through the R.A.F. umbrella as
well as to lend other fire support where needed. There was no
problem about the choice of troopships: the converted Belgian
cross-channel steamers *Prince Albert* and *Prince Leopold* were
available and ideally suited for the role. Modified to carry
American Higgins boats, the newest type of landing craft available,
these small steamers were unusually fast for troop carriers yet so

quiet-running that they stood a good chance of approaching the enemy shore undetected on a suitably dark night, no matter how still the air. 3 Commando had already ridden them into action once, during the "Claymore" landing in the Lofotens that March.

Lieutenant-Colonel Durnford-Slater arrived at Richmond Terrace the morning after Haydon's summons reached him at Largs. The staff gave him a short briefing on the over-all scheme and then he was handed the complete intelligence folder on the target area. Brigadier Haydon, who was scheduled to depart on another operation in a few days and would be gone during the most critical period of planning, wanted Durnford-Slater to stand in for him in his absence—a logical enough choice since it was he who would ultimately be charged with carrying out the plan.

"Look this over," said the Chief of Staff, "and when you're done we'll go in and see the C.C.O. He wants your opinion whether this plan is really feasible from a ground viewpoint. Let me know when you're ready to talk with him."

Left alone with the folder, Durnford-Slater studied the contents carefully. There were photographs taken by the R.A.F. reconnaissance aircraft on 29th October; these had been annotated by photograph interpreters from R.A.F. intelligence, and neatly inked circles marked the German positions. There were intelligence reports from a variety of sources, maps, transcripts of local refugee interrogations, hydrographic tables. As he scanned this material the young lieutenant-colonel felt his excitement growing. This was just the sort of operation he had been begging for! He made notes, measured distances on the maps and photographs, jotted down figures and added them up. There seemed to be no serious flaws in the ground plan.

Then he went in to see Mountbatten.

The interview was surprisingly brief. Mountbatten wanted to be very sure that the first major operation undertaken in his stewardship would be a success, but it did not take Durnford-Slater long to satisfy him.

"This all seems very ambitious," the new C.C.O. began. "Don't you think it would be better to take on something not quite so strong? How do you intend to deal with the German battery?"

Durnford-Slater replied with the assurance of a professional gunner, "Sir, if you will allow the cruiser and her attendant destroyers to close within three thousand yards and give the battery a real pounding at first light, I am sure we can dispose of that problem. You may rely upon my men to look after the German garrison.''

The other man considered this reply for a moment, then nodded his approval. It is interesting to note that from that moment forward he never again showed the least qualm about the magnitude of the project. It was probably this ability to consider all risks and objections and then, after making a decision, to commit himself so wholeheartedly that made Mountbatten as successful a commander in Whitehall as he had been on the bridge of a destroyer. By the time he retired in 1965 he headed all Britain's armed forces in his capacity of Chief of the Imperial Defence Staff.

The moment he left the C.C.O.'s office Durnford-Slater entered into a period of intense activity, hammering out the remaining details of the Vaagso raid in company with his air and naval counterparts. The biggest problem he could foresee for his own command was that of control, or to put it more simply, communication; because of the nature and location of the various tasks in the target area 3 Commando would obviously have to be fragmented, with troops and sections going off in all directions on their own particular missions. Keeping in touch with these scattered elements would be a difficult problem, as would maintaining contact with the command post on the flagship from ashore, and with the aircraft overhead from the flagship. He had brought Charley Head, 3 Commando's signals officer, down to London with him, and now he dropped these problems in his friend's lap while he set about drawing up the final ground plan in detail. There was precious little time left for staff work as the date tentatively set for the assault, 21st December, was now barely two weeks off.

John Durnford-Slater was happy during the subsequent days with their hurried pace and long hours. Not only did he have a *real* operation for his men at last, one which would finally let them sink their teeth into real German combat troops, but owing to Charles Haydon's temporary absence he had virtual *carte blanche* in making the vital decisions in planning the operation; his cup was running over.

The final scenario of the raid began to take shape. The two troopships with their warship escort would penetrate the fjord shortly before dawn. They would keep to the north side, sheltered from the German battery on Maaloy by the bulging nose of land south of the town. The two steamers would quietly lower their landing craft while the warships glided ahead to a position opposite Maaloy and took the battery under fire. Under cover of this bombardment the landing craft would approach the shore. At a signal from Durnford-Slater in the lead landing craft the bombardment would lift, ramps would go down on the designated beaches, and the commandos would rush ashore.

Three troops under Durnford-Slater would land at the edge of South Vaagso and sweep north through the town, while Jack Churchill took two troops into the battery position on Maaloy. The remaining troop under Lieutenant Bob Clement would go in near the tiny settlements of Halnoesvik and Hollevik, south-west of the town, to locate and destroy what the photograph interpreters thought to be a large gun on the hill behind the houses.

This accounted for the six troops of 3 Commando. The attached 2 Commando troop would have no specific combat mission assigned, but would constitute instead the assault force reserve, available on call wherever needed. The critical point might be in or around South Vaagso, where there was a German garrison of about 200 men, but more likely would be on Maaloy—the photographs showed quite a lot of wire entanglements around the battery position, indicating a prepared defence, and if surprise were not complete a hot fight could develop in this area.

Brigadier Haydon had considered these possibilities and wanted the reserve troop left afloat until needed; from shipboard it could proceed to any point with minimum delay. Space is at a premium on board a warship of any type, but the navy promised to make room for the extra troop somewhere aboard *Kenya;* with the admiral and the brigadier maintaining their command post on the bridge the extra troop would be right on tap, immediately responsive to the brigade commander's orders.

Because of the extreme northern latitude of the target (61° 55″ N) the hours of winter daylight are exceptionally short. During the month of December a day at Vaagso spans a little over seven hours from darkness to darkness, with sunrise and sunset barely five hours apart. Thus close timing would be critical, for certain phases of the operation offered greater chances of success in darkness but most of the fighting ashore would be better undertaken by daylight. The assault would be so timed that the landing craft would touch shore just at the first moment of "false morning".[1] All tasks ashore would have to be completed within five hours of landing in order to get the troops re-embarked and the ships clear of the fjord before full darkness. The force would then withdraw at top speed so as to be beyond effective striking range of Norwegian-based German aircraft by dawn the following day. The Luftwaffe's reaction would undoubtedly be vigorous.

Charley Head was immersed in technical plans for signalling between the various components of the raiding force. Passing by the room where the signallers held forth, Durnford-Slater was stunned to hear him talking confidently about kilocycles and wave transmissions with his knowledgeable naval counterparts. It was a new side to his friend's character, and Durnford-Slater wondered if he really knew what a kilocycle was, suspecting that he would never recognize one if he met it in Piccadilly Circus wearing a three-foot identity disc.

He need not have worried. Whatever Head may have lacked in practical experience he more than made up in plain horse sense and managerial ability; in a surprisingly short time he got himself appointed chairman of the signals planning committee and sat back to let the others argue the electronic technicalities while he simply made sure that the detailed results fitted correctly into the operational plan. Durnford-Slater relaxed. The signals plan would work.

But there were still problems enough to occupy almost everyone, and many of them took considerable ingenuity to solve.

Everyone agreed that it was desirable to approach the enemy coast under complete electronic silence, lest a stray radio or radar emission alert the enemy to the advent of the force and spoil any chance of surprising the dangerous Maaloy battery. Somehow, without radio, radar or lights, all ships would have to keep station on a pitch-dark night and maintain their exact positions relative to the leading vessel while entering the fjord; otherwise the precise timing of the opening events of the raid would come apart. Someone mentioned the towing spar, a device dating back to the days of square-rigged men-of-war, a white-painted log of irregular shape designed to create a small wake of

---

[1]Beginning morning nautical twilight, or B.M.N.T., in military and nautical terminology.

STADTLANDET

Vaagso

BREMANGERLANDET

NORDFJORD

Batalden Mt.

Floro

NORTH SEA

SOGNEFJORD

N O R W A Y

Herdla

N
W   E
S

◎ Bergen

FJORD

HARDANGER

Hardanger Vidda

**WESTERN
NORWAY**

Nautical Miles

0   5   10   15   20

its own towed behind each vessel on a measured length of line.
The bow lookout on each ship keeps the spar of the ship ahead in
sight at all times and if the ship itself fades from view directs the
helmsman of his own vessel, thereby keeping station exactly.
This seemed a neat enough solution, so word went out to the
shipfitters at Scapa to attach the requisite cables and drums on
the fantails of all ships of the "Archery" force.

Another problem had to do with ensuring an accurate
landfall before leaving the safety of the open sea, for one
opening in the Norwegian coastline looks about like any other by
night, and there are dozens of inlets within thirty miles of the
entrance to Nordfjord. If there were the slightest error in the
dead-reckoning navigation required on the last leg of the journey,
the force could very well sail right into the wrong fjord or
between the wrong two islands in the dark, either running itself
aground in unfamiliar waters or getting trapped in a cul-de-sac at
dawn with the Luftwaffe overhead. There did not seem to be any
obvious solution to this one except precise navigation and careful
briefing on how to recognize landmarks around the right fjord
entrance. The Royal Navy planning representatives frowned and
turned to the next problem.

Navigation in the *Indreled* is a tricky enough business by
day, and attempting a surreptitious passage during the hours of
darkness only multiplies the difficulties. The waters vary in
depth as much as do the surrounding mountains in height, and
just as rapidly; a ship may have thirty fathoms under her keel one
moment and tear out her bottom on a concealed rock the next.
Experienced pilots graduated from a long and demanding appren-
ticeship con the vessels which ply these waters in peacetime,
and lighthouses mark the channels by night. But pilots with an
intimate knowledge of obscure continental waterways did not
abound in wartime London, and if any at all were around no one
had ever thought to compile a list. The Germans had probably
blacked out the lighthouses, or at least "diddled" the marking
system in some way so as to prevent their use as navigational
checkpoints. The only answer seemed to lie in locating qualified
and trustworthy pilots. Advertising for them too openly was out
of the question, for fear of compromising the operation; any
inquiries would have to be made with great discretion. Perhaps
Kompani Linge might know of someone? Martin Linge was
contacted, and promised to do his best.

The German lookout station on Husevaago at the mouth of

Nordfjord presented perhaps the knottiest problem. Surprise was the key to overcoming the Maaloy battery, and surprise depended on getting past the lookout post undetected. Since the ships would have to pass within 1,500 yards of the enemy sentinels this meant their attention had to be surely and positively diverted elsewhere during those critical minutes. Approaching the target from the north was out of the question, for the ships would then have to sail right under the guns of the Halsoer battery and down the length of Ulvesund with its populated shores. Besides, there was a rumour (later proved untrue) that the Germans had mined the northern approach. There was nothing for it but to go in past Husevaago, and have the R.A.F. lay on some kind of a diversion to keep the German lookouts entertained while the ships slipped by.

Although the Halsoer battery would be unable to bring fire on the ships in Vaagsfjord because of the masking effect of the intervening mountain, it still represented a threat to the landing force because it had its own infantry platoon attached and could conceivably send reinforcements into South Vaagso at an inopportune time. And there is no law against using artillerymen as infantry in a tight spot when their guns cannot be brought to bear. Durnford-Slater wanted to employ an extra half-troop (which he was certain Brigadier Haydon would agree to loan him from somewhere within the brigade) to set up a roadblock well north of South Vaagso, cutting the lone coastal road against the transfer of reinforcements from Halsoer. But how to get the half-troop there in time? Although the Onslow-class destroyers drew less than sixteen feet of water, thus having the capability of negotiating the shallow passage between the Maaloy battery and South Vaagso, some of the naval officers felt this would be too risky; but after Admiral Burrough pointed out that the only real risk was from the Maaloy battery, it was agreed to hold the half-troop on board one of the Onslows and to run through the strait as soon as the battery was silenced. The destroyer with all its armament could presumably suppress any small-arms fire from the Germans in the town itself as it steamed by the waterfront.

The German battery on Rugsundo Island, four miles eastward down Nordfjord, was another factor to be taken into consideration while planning the assault. It was sited where it could easily bring observed fire on the entire Maaloy-South Vaagso area, and was allegedly equipped with even heavier guns

than the Maaloy battery. The Rugsundo battery would constitute
a particular threat to the naval elements of the force, as the
vessels would be unable to take much evasive action in the
confined waters of the fjord. The air planners promised to deal
with this battery at the start of the action. Indeed, an air raid on
Rugsundo would probably make the ideal distraction to fix all
German eyes up-fjord during the penetration of the fjord and
passage of the lookout station, and if their high explosives failed
to dismount the guns a few smoke bombs would at least blind the
observers.

The skeletal plan, gradually fleshing out with details, was
beginning to take shape. But if the problems encountered by the
naval and military planners were complex, those faced by the
R.A.F. representatives were nightmarish.

In the early days of the war Britain's very survival had
clearly depended upon R.A.F.'s Fighter Command, and first
priority for aircraft production necessarily went to the speedy
short-range interceptors of the Hurricane and Spitfire series needed
to defend her cities. Subsequently counter-attack became the
watchword, and the emphasis was shifted to heavy bombers
capable of reaching industrial targets deep inside Germany itself.
Until only recently there had been no clear-cut requirement for
long-range fighters, and the first aircraft of this type—the Bristol
Beaufighter—was just beginning to roll off the assembly lines.
But few of these machines had yet reached the operational
squadrons of Coastal Command, so there were not many aircraft
capable of providing air cover to a force operating as far from
home bases as Vaagso.

The basic problem of the air planners was that of keeping
the Luftwaffe off the "Archery" force during the entire day of
the raid. This involved solving a bevy of smaller problems:
scheduling of sorties, long-range navigation by night over open
water to arrive over an exact point at a precise moment, a critical
shortage of air navigation charts of the Norwegian coast, and the
biggest problem of all—finding enough aircraft with the requisite
operational range.

The obvious answer to this last was to move the home bases
nearer to the target by using Fleet Air Arm fighters operating off
one of the two aircraft carriers then sheltering at Scapa Flow.
The C.C.O. planning committee had in fact considered this
possibility earlier and broached the subject to the Chiefs of Staff
Committee, who firmly turned down the idea: capital ships

Hurricane

would not—repeat *not*—be risked on small-scale combined operations into areas where the enemy enjoyed air superiority. So the problem of air cover had been turned right back to the R.A.F.

The intelligence specialists were able to put up a fairly accurate estimate of Luftwaffe strength in central Norway. Within striking distance of Vaagso their file showed thirty-three bomber and reconnaissance aircraft at Stavanger and another nine at Trondheim, about 50 per cent of these machines being operationally serviceable at any given time. A squadron of Me-109 fighters located at Herdla aerodrome, about eighty miles down the coast towards Bergen, could be over Vaagso in about an hour's notice, although their limited fuel capacity would forbid their remaining long over the target. There were more of these fighters at Stavanger and Trondheim, and although these bases were beyond operational range of Vaagso for the Me-109, the planes could be brought into action by making a refuelling stop at Herdla *en route*. Clearly Herdla was the key to local air superiority; if it were knocked out no German fighters could reach the target area and the R.A.F. fighter umbrella (if one could be devised) should then be able to meet with other German intruders on favourable terms.

The problem of Herdla was referred to the Chiefs of Staff Committee with a request for assistance from Bomber Command. In a short time word came back from Air Chief Marshal Sir Wilfred Freeman that the committee had allocated three Bomber Command Stirlings each to Herdla and Stavanger aerodromes for an early-morning strike on the day of the raid. This was good news, but just to be sure of keeping Herdla non-operational through the day the chief air planner on the C.C.O. committee, Group Captain A. H. Willetts, laid on a follow-up strike at noon by Blenheim bombers of Number 114 and 110 Squadrons, Coastal Command, as well as a strike against coastal shipping in the Stavanger area to draw off more of the German fighter strength.

There were only two British fighter bases within striking distance of Vaagso, one at Wick on the extreme northern tip of Scotland and the other at Sumburgh in the Shetland Islands. Fortuitously, Coastal Command already had a few squadrons of the new Beaufighters and a number of Blenheim fighters, a rebuilt version of the old Blenheim bomber, too clumsy to be much good in air-to-air combat but at least having enough fuel capacity for a round trip to Norway—at these very bases. By committing all the aircraft at these bases on a continuous schedule it just might be possible to keep an air umbrella over Vaagso through the day.

Vaagso is about 250 nautical miles from Sumburgh and over 400 from Wick, so roughly half each aircraft's fuel would be consumed just in getting there and—hopefully—getting back. This meant that almost immediately after each sortie reached the target, the next would have to depart from base to relieve it on station. The timing would be close and there would be little margin for error but it could be done, just barely. Willetts and his chief assistant, Wing-Commander R. J. Oxley, D.F.D., told the planning committee to count on air cover.

The raid on Rugsundo to knock out the battery and distract the German coast-watchers was assigned to the Hampden bombers of Number 50 Squadron. The Hampden was one of the oddest-looking machines in the R.A.F. inventory; its fuselage consisted of a high thin pod connected to the tail surfaces by a slender boom so that it resembled nothing so much as a frying-pan turned on edge with a wing surface grafted across the top; but its two engines could lift a ton of bombs to the target. A strike by a swarm of these startling-looking machines should

Bristol Blenheim

create enough excitement to keep all German eyes up-fjord at the critical moment and might even do a great deal of damage to the battery. But the navigation and timing were going to be tricky on a black night.

The five remaining squadrons at Wick and Sumburgh, Numbers 404, 254, 235, 236 and 248, were equipped with a mixture of the agile new Beaufighters and the staggering old Blenheims. They would be the fighter umbrella itself. The swift and manoeuvrable Beaus would probably fare well enough against anything the Germans could put up, but if Bomber Command failed to put Herdla out of business the crews of the unwieldy Blenheims would need a lot of luck as well as skill.

At the end of two days of intense activity the details of the "Archery" plan had pretty well fallen into place. Durnford-Slater had divided his landing force into five major groups and numbered them for planning and control purposes:

> *Group I,* Lieutenant Clement's Number 2 Troop, would land at Hollevik under Clement's command and clear the Hollevik-Halnoesvik area where the extra gun had been reported, then move up the coastal road to South Vaagso and form a reserve for Group II unless given other orders.

> *Group II,* under Durnford-Slater himself, would consist of Captain Bradley's Number 1 Troop to secure the landing place and do the main demolitions, and Captain Giles' and Captain Forrester's 3 and 4 Troops as assault elements. This group would land immediately south of South Vaagso, sweep northward through the town, and perform most of the industrial dirty work.

> *Group III,* under Major Churchill, would consist of Captain Ronald's 5 Troop and Captain Young's 6 Troop and would assault Maaloy, knocking out the German battery and then going on to clear the entire island.

> *Group IV,* would be the floating reserve troop from Number 2 Commando and would remain aboard *Kenya.*

> *Group V,* the extra half troop borrowed from Number 2 Commando, would land from *Oribi* on the west shore of Ulvesund, set up a roadblock between South and North Vaagso, and send a fighting patrol into the latter town in search of stray Germans.

The portions of the ground plan that must be done in Richmond Terrace were complete now, so Durnford-Slater and Head boarded an evening train for Largs to start getting 3 Commando ready for the projected operation. They carried a huge packing case with them containing a beautifully detailed scale model of the entire Vaagso area (courtesy of the R.A.F. photograph intelligence service), and because of its bulk and the secret nature of the contents they had a compartment all to themselves. They were acutely conscious that the information they carried was of great potential value to the enemy: the normal hazards of such a raid were acceptable, but the idea of a German reception committee standing by at each of the chosen landing points was not much of an aid to digestion. In this condition of mild tension it created a nervous moment in the middle of the night to have the door to their compartment suddenly burst open and a man lunge in. But the interloper proved to be nothing more than a drunken sailor searching for a card game.

The next day at Largs Durnford-Slater briefed Jack Churchill on the general details of the operation, omitting only the name of the target area. Then he left the operational preparation in Churchill's hands while he himself went off to Scapa Flow to talk with Admiral Tovey.

He was met at pierside by the Admiral's barge, which carried him in unaccustomed pomp to the flagship of the Home Fleet, H.M.S. *King George V*, where he was conducted to the Admiral's cabin.

Admiral Tovey had a scale drawing of the objective before him and was obviously well-acquainted with the operational plan. They exchanged the customary greetings, and then the older man began questioning him about details of the ground plan.

"Where do you propose to land the men going into the town?"

Durnford-Slater showed him the Group II landing point on the map—a rough stretch of rocks at the base of a low cliff just south of the Seternes lighthouse. The Admiral demurred.

"Wouldn't this be a better place to go in?" he asked, pointing to a small cove a short distance up the coast. "It's not nearly so steep a slope to tackle once you get ashore. I should think you'd want to move out as fast as possible from the landing point."

Durnford-Slater shook his head.

"That place would be under too much machine-gun fire, sir. Besides, my men have been practising cliff landings for a long time now." He went on to outline Forrester's cliff assault drill, concluding: "Actually, the cliff is the *best* landing point just because it's the last place the enemy would expect us. We ought to take him completely by surprise."

The admiral nodded and sat back.

"Very well, Slater, we shall do our best to land you there. But it's a rough spot and it may be impossible to get the boats right up to the beach. Your men are probably going to have to swim the last bit."

"We've done that before, sir," Durnford-Slater grinned, "and we can do it again."

At this point the phone on the admiral's desk buzzed and he picked it up. A lengthy conversation ensued, after which he hung up and looked speculatively at Durnford-Slater.

"Just one more thing," he said. "That was the Prime Minister. What am I going to tell him if the operation turns out a failure?"

"There will be no failure, sir," replied Durnford-Slater. "We shall carry it off."

The admiral smiled and dismissed him. Like Mountbatten, he had needed to gauge for himself the spirit of the men who would actually execute the plan. Having satisfied himself on this score, he would support it in every way possible.

The following day found Durnford-Slater back in London. At Richmond Terrace he learned that S.O.E. had come through with permission for its Norwegian company to take part in the raid, so he hurried over to Kingston House to see Martin Linge. His pleasure at greeting his friend quickly turned to horror. The Norwegian officers were openly discussing the most secret details of the operation.

It was always impossible to keep the actual location of objectives in Norway from these men, for invariably someone would recognize terrain features or a street pattern or the shape of a harbour the minute he saw the planning map. Now "Vågsøy" and Måløyna", names thus far restricted to the closely-guarded confines of the C.O.H.Q. briefing room, figured prominently in the conversation.

Durnford-Slater cautioned Linge about the dangers of loose talk, but the Norwegian was unperturbed.

"We talk freely within this building," he said, "but you needn't worry about what any of these fellows say elsewhere. They are all very discreet."

Shuddering, Durnford-Slater shook hands with him and departed.

7

MISSION UNKNOWN

When Durnford-Slater first returned from London with news of the impending operation, Jack Churchill's immediate reaction was one of polite interest but no very great enthusiasm. Having been in the commandos from the start, he had seen all too many of these plans prepared, troops briefed, special training and rehearsal exercises run off, and sometimes even the men loaded aboard ship. Almost invariably the operations were cancelled for one reason or another, usually at the last possible minute, and morale plummeted as everyone went back to routine training.

To 3 Commando's new second-in-command, the reasons given for these cancellations usually sounded like thinly veiled excuses for doing nothing, a practice which he considered the besetting military sin. Roger Keyes had been peremptorily relieved of his duties as Director of Combined Operations for expressing this same view loudly and frequently in higher councils, but no one at such rarified levels really cared too much what majors thought so Churchill's dark mutterings went unnoticed.

Left in charge of the final preparations at Largs, he now made two resolutions: he would not announce to the unit that an operation was in the offing, so as to limit the number of persons who would be disappointed when it got cancelled; and he would run a few pet training schemes of his own devising to sharpen the odd skills needed for this particular operation, just in case it did *not* get cancelled. Time enough for briefing the troops on shipboard, if they ever got that far; in the meantime, let them build up extra proficiency in those arts of greatest potential value against a surprised German garrison in the cold Norwegian dawn.

So the troopers at Largs found themselves lying on their bellies late at night on an icy Scottish beach, firing at man-sized targets which seemed to duck and bob in the shadows cast by drifting parachute flares. At dawn they were out again, peering down the sights of their rifles at dim targets faintly seen in the distance through coils of barbed wire. They hurled grenades into foxholes and rain-barrels and through dummy window-frames around a "championship course" and hotly disputed their scores over beer in the evening.

Everywhere they went the compact figure of their second-in-command was in evidence; again and again they found that their best was not good enough for him. When he examined shot groups in the rifle targets and found a lance-corporal had not zeroed his rifle correctly, he would point out that from the same range his longbow was more accurate, and offer to prove it. He was always on hand to demonstrate the best way to parry a bayonet thrust, or to administer a merciless tongue-lashing to the hapless trooper who reported his rifle "jammed" when he had in fact forgotten to release the safety catch. At night he created a horrible racket in a Largs hotel with his beloved bagpipe while a few unfortunate souls who had planned to retire early tossed sleeplessly on their beds and cursed beneath their breath.

Anytine he had a captive audience he expounded his own military axioms:

"There's nothing worse than sitting on your bum bottom doing nothing just because the enemy happens to leave you alone for a moment while he has a go at the unit on your flank. Pitch in and support your neighbour any way you can, because if he meets with success it's going to make your own job that much easier when the time comes." Or:

"Always remember to aim low when you're shooting in light this dim. Even if you overdo it a little you're apt to bounce one into the Hun, and a ricochet will tear him up even worse than a clean hit. Have a look at the second target over there if you don't believe me." Or:

"Our own operations won't always go according to plan. Don't forget that the enemy has plans of his own. When this happens, improvise. Tell the chaps on your left and right what support you need from them and what you propose to do. Then *do* it. The big thing is to react quickly. Recover the initiative and keep moving."

It was refreshing. The men in the ranks, most of whom had heretofore known "Mad Jack" only by reputation, were fascinated by his breezy way of expressing himself and his sometimes unorthodox ways of going about things. But orthodox or not, he made good sense, and it did not take any competent soldier long to realize it. Spirits sagging from the long period of inactivity began to pick up again.

Something was in the wind; that too was apparent. Major Churchill may have resolved not to get their hopes too high by talking about the operation, but the men were not fooled; troops can sense it when their officers know something they do not. Nor did it take a Sherlock Holmes to observe which way all the training schemes pointed, and to draw some fairly obvious conclusions: a night cliff landing, followed by a dawn assault on prepared enemy positions and a chance to meet some Germans face-to-face. The prospect was debated among friends, and sizeable wagers made on the general location of the objective.

All leaves for December had suddenly been cancelled. That was a good sign, too.

Of course a few key members of the unit had had to be let in on certain portions of the secret but Durnford-Slater, a zealous exponent of security, had told them only as much as they needed to know to do their own jobs. Captain "Slinger" Martin, the administrative officer, was already compiling lists of necessary equipment and visiting the depots to draw extra sweaters, wool mufflers and ammunition. The adjutant, Alan Smallman, closeted himself with Churchill and Lieutenant Head, working out the exact details to go in the operations order Durnford-Slater had outlined for each troop. Doctor Sam Corry and his orderlies packed extra medical supplies into carrying kits and turned them over to Martin for shipment.

Durnford-Slater returned from Scapa in good spirits, and on the 13th December Number 3 Commando travelled quietly but jubilantly to Gourock. Tied up alongside the quay were two familiar shapes: *Prince Charles* and *Prince Leopold,* with seamen bustling about their decks and a feather of steam showing at the funnel. Troop commanders lined up their men for a final nose-count and the commando embarked. Then the gangways came up and without ceremony the two Belgian steamers cast off and pointed their prows towards the Orkneys and Scapa Flow.

On board there was almost a holiday spirit. Of course Christmas was coming, but no one thought about that; the cause of all the exultation was the sense of impending action. Aside from the very few officers who had already been briefed, the embarked commandos still did not know where they were going or exactly what they were supposed to do when they got there.

But one thing was certain: they looked forward to going there
and doing it.

8

FINAL REHEARSALS

By 15th December most of the naval force was assembled at
Scapa Flow and those commando elements who were to travel to
Vaagso aboard other ships had been transferred from *Prince
Albert* and *Prince Leopold*. Brigadier Haydon had not yet returned
from Operation "Kitbag", Number 6 Commando's assault on
the German coast defence installations at Floro, about twenty-
five miles south of Vaagso. The landing was to be made that day
and everyone was anxiously waiting for news.

But Admiral Burrough was already at Scapa, and conference followed conference on the flagship with bewildering frequency.
Every foreseeable problem was brought up for discussion by the
staff, solutions were debated at length and contingency plans laid
out.

Some Number 2 Commando types arrived on the scene via
the Orkney Ferry—4 Troop under Captain R. H. "Dickie"
Hooper and half of 6 Troop under Captain David Birney—and
were greeted with friendly jeering as they came up the gangways.
A few stray members of other commandos also came aboard,
mostly medical orderlies and signalmen.

In the midst of this flurry of activity news of the utter failure
of the "Kitbag" raid burst like a bombshell. The raiding force
had made its way across the North Sea undetected and edged
close to Floro during the hours of darkness. The appointed time
for landing was just over an hour away, and lookouts on the ships
could see what appeared to be the final checkpoint, Batalden,
looming faintly against the skyline. Then, to the disgust of the
embarked commandos, the fleet suddenly turned around and
went home, without making contact with the enemy.

What had actually happened was very simple. The Force
Navigator was unable to guarantee his exact position after the

final hours of steaming across rough seas on an overcast night; he felt sure his dead reckoning had been accurate but had no sure way of checking it, and although the landfall looked like Batalden as it had been described to him and as it appeared on the charts there was still an element of doubt; as already noted, one point on the mountainous Norwegian coast looks about like any other when seen dimly from the sea through a pair of night glasses. Unwilling to risk his force on an uncertain landfall, the Naval Commander refused to land the landing force and ordered the ships to turn around. An attached *Kompani Linge* soldier who was a native of the immediate area sighted had indeed been Batalden, but no one had thought to consult him at the critical moment and the opportunity passed.

The net loss of "Kitbag", aside from the abysmal waste of time and effort in its preparation, amounted to six commandos killed and eleven seriously wounded in the accidental explosion of a grenade on board ship. Some of the casualties were from *Kompani Linge*. Brigadier Haydon and his Brigade Major, the distinguished novelist Robert Henriques, returned to Scapa in an agony of frustration.

Admiral Burrough called his staff together once more. The regrettable affair at Floro only served to emphasize the necessity of making an absolutely accurate landfall and being able to confirm it beyond any reasonable doubt. He had every confidence in the navigation of his flag captain, Captain Michael Denny, R.N. But suppose "Archery", too, ran into bad weather during the final hours of the approach and Denny could not get a star sight? A positive solution must be found.

There was some discussion of marker buoys, and who could lay one accurately and when, and whether planting a buoy at the fjord mouth before the arrival of the main force would not give the whole show away. And then the obvious solution appeared: a submarine. Why not send out a sub in advance to locate the fjord entrance, confirm it by periscope sighting, then lie doggo on the bottom through the night preceding the raid and surface just as the force arrived, thus serving as the marker buoy itself? An urgent message went off to the Admiralty and was soon in the hands of the Commander-in-Chief, Submarines: could he make one of his craft available to serve as a final navigational checkpoint for the "Archery" force?

At dawn on the 17th December the force carried out a full-scale rehearsal, designated as "Exercise L", within the fleet anchorage at Scapa Flow. The objective was a small island whose shape and general conformation closely seconded that of the Vaagso–Maaloy area. *Kenya* and her escorting destroyers went through the motions of laying down the preliminary bombardment, and as the Higgins boats carrying the men of 3 Commando approached the shore a flight of Hampdens led by Group Captain Willetts swept in to drop smoke floats in front of the landing points. Watched only by the black-faced sheep who inhabited the island, the commandos stormed ashore with a shout and fanned out towards their designated objectives.

Although only a selected few of the officers and none of the men participating had yet heard the name or seen so much as a sketch map of Vaagso, the exercise objective chosen for each troop corresponded closely with its actual objective at Vaagso, both from the point of view of conformation of the ground and in terms of distance from the landing point. The water was very cold and the men, forced to wade ashore because the landing craft could not reach the rocky beachline, returned to their ships at the end of the exercise with chattering teeth and numb feet, dripping wet. A few odds and ends of equipment had been lost, including about twenty steel helmets, and there was a last-minute flurry to recover or replace the missing items.

After the rehearsal was completed the major commanders gathered on the flagship to critique the action and discuss tactical lessons. The experimental smoke floats dropped by the Hampdens were acclaimed a complete success, having masked the landing points from view during the moment of debarking, and they were written into the final plan. With this extra protection everyone felt that casualties during the landing would be far less severe.

There was one great flaw in "Exercise L". A number of key communications personnel had not arrived at Scapa in time to take part. Charley Head's signals committee was not yet satisfied that all would go smoothly. In particular, the deck-to-air radio link for talking with the R.A.F. fighters high above the flagship had not been tested, and if the Luftwaffe managed to intervene this link could be a vital one.

D–Day for the operation was set back to 26th December, and a second rehearsal ("Exercise L2") was laid on for the morning of the 22nd to check out small changes in timing and to allow the communicators a chance to try out their apparatus. The Coastal Command squadrons who would actually provide fighter cover during the operation were asked to put up a few aircraft in order to verify the deck-to-air link but were unable to do so; however, Coastal Command promised to provide its own liaison party to sail aboard the flagship and would brief them on the signal procedures to be followed so there should be no problem.

Unfortunately the weather deteriorated and "L2" did not come off as planned; much of the problem play had to be eliminated at the last minute. In the interval between exercises *Kenya* and the Hampdens of Number 50 Squadron went off and conducted a private exercise of their own to perfect the co-ordination and timing of air and naval elements of the preliminary bombardment. In the final reduced-scale "L2" they conducted a "dry run" in which the timing worked out flawlessly. No troops took part in this exercise.

The Admiralty had meanwhile approved the use of a submarine as a marker buoy and Lieutenant-Commander M. K. Cavanagh-Mainwaring, D.S.O., the master of H.M.S. *Tuna,* a new, fast fleet submarine then lying at Scapa, came aboard *Kenya* for instructions. Admiral Burrough turned him over to the "Archery" planning staff, who briefed him on *Tuna*'s proposed role in the operation. Together they worked out a simple short-range communication system using *Kenya*'s asdic (an underwater sound-detection system installed on all warships) to preserve radio silence while approaching the objective; the signals were made by the simple expedient of rapping on the hulls of the two ships with a hammer. After a quick rehearsal of the challenge and countersign to be used, *Tuna* slipped quietly out of the fleet anchorage at ten o'clock on the morning of the 23rd.

The final rehearsal had been completed and all troops isolated aboard ship. At last the veil of secrecy surrounding the operation was lifted. Officers received detailed maps and diagrams of the objective, with the place names filled in. For the first time the members of 3 Commando found out where they were going. Durnford-Slater had brought along the large-scale model made by the R.A.F. photograph reconnaissance experts and now it went the rounds, passing from ship to ship. Troop officers conducted detailed briefings for their men. Sufficient time was allotted for each section to gather around the model and examine it closely. Troop and section leaders asked questions of their men:

"Fray, what objective has been assigned to your section?"

"Robinson, show me the route by which we approach our second objective."

Short Stirling

"What happens if your section leader is wounded, killed, lost, etcetera?"

"Habron, what is the objective of the troop on our right?"

As the force began preparing for sea a very disturbing signal came in from London. At the Chiefs of Staff meeting on the morning of the 23rd the six Stirlings previously allotted for the preliminary strikes to knock out Herdla and Stavanger aerodromes had been cancelled. The decision was by no means a capricious one—the change of date for the landings had brought this commitment into conflict with others having a justifiably higher priority at Bomber Command—but it spelt trouble for the Beaufighter squadrons of the air umbrella and mortal danger for the Blenheims. It would be touch-and-go trying to keep the Luftwaffe away from the "Archery" force now.

Coastal Command still had its own follow-up raid on Herdla set to go in at noon but the timing could not be advanced for a number of reasons. The misgivings of the military and naval planners over the untried radio-telephone net linking the flagship to the fighters grew deeper.

A last-minute visitor to the force at Scapa was Admiral Mountbatten himself. After conferring briefly with the principal commanders on board *Kenya* the C.C.O. was piped aboard the

troopships where he spoke to the assembled commandos, expressing
his confidence in their success and wishing them good hunting.

"One last thing," he told them. "When my ship, the
destroyer *Kelly,* went down off Crete early this year the Germans
machine-gunned the survivors in the water. There's absolutely no
need to treat them gently on my account. Good luck to all of
you."

9

STORMY CROSSING

At 2115 hours on Christmas Eve the seven ships of the "Archery"
force upped anchor and sailed out of Scapa Flow. The destination
of the first leg of the trip was Sollum Voe, a small base in the
Shetlands whence the final run-in of some three hundred miles
would be made the following night.

The weather forecasters had been pessimistic, and with
good reason. Within a few hours after leaving port the ships
began to pitch and roll violently. The wind and seas rose with
frightening speed and soon a full gale was blowing, with winds
at force 8 on the Beaufort scale. The two troopships laboured
particularly heavily as waves crashed over their decks; hull plates
groaned and screeched in protest against the cruel strain as the
ships flexed over the wave crests.

"I was sitting in the wardroom after supper," recorded
Captain Martin, 3 Commando's middle-aged administrative officer,
"playing 'Pontoon' with Bill Bradley, Bill Etches, and Algy
Forrester. The ship started rocking and rolling; we continued to
play for a while as other people disappeared to their cabins. I had
just called 'Twist!' when the ship gave a tremendous lurch and I
found myself sprawling on the floor with Algy Forrester. I was
then beginning to feel a bit heady as was everyone else. Bill
Etches went, I followed, then Algy and Bill Bradley.

"It was with some difficulty that I made my way to my
cabin, which I shared with the ship's doctor. The ship was
heeling and reeling in the teeth of the gale, becoming more

violent every minute that passed. Gripping hard at anything stable, I managed at the third attempt to heave myself into my bunk.

"The ship was heeling over at an alarming angle, much beyond the safety angle which her designers allowed for; crashes and bumps were heard continuously as the seas buffeted the ship like a cockleshell. The cabin very soon was a shambles. Shaving gear, clothes, equipment, everything was mixed up on the floor and rolling about. I was very sick. This frightening experience went on all through the night."

At one point the captain of *Prince Charles*, Commander Fell, was invited below by his secretary to witness a strange phenomenon. A writing desk in the corner of a forward compartment was moving rhythmically up and down the wall a distance of some six inches. It was an eerie effect and might have led lesser men to acknowledge the existence of poltergeists, but Fell and his secretary investigated and found the cause to be the heavy seas pressing in on the bows flexing the foreward bulkhead against which the desk was fastened.

The warships were built to endure heavy weather, but even they endured such a battering that the officer commanding the destroyer escort, Captain Armstrong of *Onslow,* finally sent a message to the admiral requesting a reduction in speed, which was approved immediately.

The storm abated somewhat at dawn, but considerable damage had already been done. The two troopships had taken the worst of it, and both were leaking dangerously, with about a foot of water sloshing about in the troop compartments; the little steamers were wallowing low in the water, maintaining headway with difficulty.

Around noon on Christmas Day the ships finally entered calmer waters and the commandos who immediately poked their noses above deck discovered that they were now in the shelter of a cluster of barren and snow-covered islands: the Shetlands. At 1300 the force dropped anchor in the tiny bay at Sollum Voe and repair parties set to work on the damaged ships. Catalina aircraft appeared overhead and alighted on the water beside the ships, carrying tools and spares. Soon the banging of hammers and the popping hiss of acetylene torches could be heard throughout the anchorage.

Martin Linge came on board *Kenya* at Sollum, bringing with him a genuine *Indreled* pilot he had somehow located in the

Catalina

Shetlands. Captain Denny conferred with the man and learned that although he had frequently conned medium-sized vessels through the waters around Vaagso he had never handled anything so large as *Kenya*. In the narrow and treacherous waters of the fjord his first experience of manoeuvring a large vessel would be somewhat analogous to that of a motorist driving in heavy traffic the first time he operates a car with power steering, but at least he knew the contours of the fjord bottom and seemed reasonably bright.

Brigadier Haydon and Admiral Burrough made a tour of the seven ships in the harbour, the admiral wanting to see the damage at first hand so as to get a better idea of the extent of repairs they would need, and the brigadier to judge his men's fighting fitness after the frightening and exhausting night at sea.

For some time the brigade had been conducting "sea experience voyages". Whenever there was a lull in training a section or sometimes a whole troop of commandos would be sent out on a short voyage in a small ship. Perhaps they would ride aboard a destroyer escort going out to meet a convoy inbound from America, or they might accompany the crew of a motor torpedo boat on a patrol off the Channel Islands. The whole purpose was to make them feel at home on small ships in rough water, for the commando soldier must be able to step off a wave-tossed vessel in condition to fight and sailors know that susceptibility to seasickness declines with experience at sea. A few of the men remarked wryly (and predictably) that it does not take practice to feel really miserable, but the "seasick trips" provided a welcome break in routine and in practice became very popular.

H.M.S. *Chiddingfold* **(Hunt Class)**

They went to *Prince Charles* first. The ship had taken on approximately 120 tons of water and almost everything forward of the superstructure was flooded to a depth of fourteen feet. As far aft as the first funnel every deck between charthouse and waterline had taken in water in varying degrees; it stood to the level of the doorsill in the sergeants' mess and the wardroom. The occupants of four cabins on C deck had been flooded out, but every accommodation was wet. Waves crashing head-on into the bows, tending to pinch them together, had dished the first two bulkheads, thus narrowing the wardroom; the fo'c'sle guard rails were stove in, and sprung rivets and leaking pipes had let the contents of the fresh water storage tanks go foul with brackish salt water. These would have to be repaired, pumped dry and refilled before anyone could have a drink.

The brigadier found the commandos on board cheerful and confident, apparently none the worse for wear. Many had been violently sick the previous night, but had recovered rapidly enough once the ship entered calmer water.

The admiral ordered *Chiddingfold* alongside to help pump out the flooded compartments. Then he and Haydon went on to *Prince Leopold*. The situation on *Leopold* was much like that on *Prince Charles*. On deck, ladders and rails were bent and wire reels and Flotta nets had been washed overboard. The heavy bulkhead under the gun platform had buckled under the pounding of the seas on the bows. The whole forepeak including the rope locker had been flooded and a horrible tangle of water-soaked lines resembling nothing so much as an explosion in an Olympian spaghetti factory floated in the oily water, blocking access to the steam ejector valves; every bit of stowed cordage had washed free of its battens.

Troop leaders reported that the seasick commandos on board *Prince Leopold* had recovered as fast as had their comrades on *Prince Charles;* the brigadier was well satisfied. Leading Seaman Gillam dived into the flooded rope locker and somehow fought through the soggy tangle to open the steam ejector valves. This probably relieved the chief engineer even more than it did the boilers.

By the time they returned to *Kenya* a new weather forecast was waiting for the admiral. It was bad news: the forecasters were giving the storm at least another twelve hours to run, possibly eighteen.

Repairs were not yet completed, and dusk was falling. If the force were to sail that night it must do so immediately. But could the troopships stand another night of battering in their present condition?

Admiral Burrough made his decision. From a naval standpoint it was imperative that the raid be postponed another twenty-four hours. There were already enough marginal factors without taking on the effects of more severe foul weather during the run-in.

Brigadier Haydon accepted the admiral's decision without hesitation; had their positions been reversed he would probably have made the same decision himself. D–Day was now fixed for the 27th December, and messages went out to Whitehall and Scapa immediately. Coastal Command was advised of the change in plan and aircrews received the word to stand down. A "blind" radio message went out to *Tuna*, already in position at the mouth of Nordfjord.

So the raiding force ate its Christmas dinner in the peaceful anchorage of Sollum Voe, and everyone got a good night's sleep to offset the effects of the previous night at sea.

Throughout the 26th Admiral Burrough waited impatiently for a new forecast. Far to the north Number 6 Commando had gone ashore as scheduled at Reine, and Admiral Hamilton was sharing Burrough's impatience to get on with the job at Vaagso; he was depending on "Archery" to draw the Luftwaffe's main strength in Norway away from "Anklet", which had no air cover at all.

As the day wore on the weather showed little change. The storm outside the anchorage raged unabated. At last, late in the afternoon, a yeoman of signals handed the admiral the long-awaited signal: every indication pointed towards the storm dying rapidly during the night, with fair weather on the morrow. The admiral and the brigadier conferred briefly and another signal went out to the Admiralty: "Archery" would be launched as scheduled at dawn on 27th December.

The troop and section leaders held their final councils of war in the wardrooms during the late afternoon and Captain Martin, who had spent the day checking the stores prepacked in the landing craft and replacing damaged demolition charges, completed his inspection. The shipfitters withdrew at last, declaring all vessels seaworthy. Everything was in readiness.

At four o'clock in the afternoon of Friday, 26th December, the force upped anchor and sailed out into the still-turbulent seas between the Shetlands and Norway.

There would be no turning back now. "Archery" was under way.

Once more the forecasters won top marks. As the force disappeared into the gathering darkness—*Kenya* in the van, followed by *Chiddingfold,* then the troopships with the Onslow-class destroyers prowling about their flanks and rear like sheep-dogs tending the flock—the wind began to fade perceptibly. Although the two transports suffered some damage at first (this time it was *Prince Leopold*'s turn to find water leaking into the troop accommodations and fresh-water tanks polluted), a few hours after midnight the skies began to clear and the sea fell calm. Fewer commandos had been seasick this time and even they recovered quickly enough to get a few hours' sleep.

Captain Denny, the force navigator, spent most of the night on his bridge, checking and rechecking his position on the charts. He was the man who would make or break the raid now. Early in the morning the skies began to clear and he was able to get occasional star sightings to check his dead-reckoning figures. Everything seemed to be in order.

At four in the morning the troops were roused from their bunks. Someone had once told Durnford-Slater that sailors made a point of wearing clean underclothing into battle so as to minimize the danger of infection in case they are wounded, and he had carefully hoarded a complete change of clean clothing since leaving Largs. Now he dressed himself carefully in fresh garments from the skin out.

Breakfast was at five, no one felt seasick any longer, and excitement was running high. At the conclusion of the meal each member of the landing force received a small haversack ration to do him for lunch, but in most cases these rations would be carried back aboard ship untouched; there would be little time for eating in the middle of the German garrison.

The asdic operator on *Kenya* reported to the bridge that he had a possible submarine contact dead ahead. A moment later he added that the sub was answering his tapped-out signals using the prearranged code. *Tuna* was bang on station and Captain Denny had brought the force arrow-straight from Sollum Voe to the mouth of the fjord.

A few minutes later *Kenya*'s bow lookout sang out. *Tuna*

was in sight, lying with her decks awash and her conning tower high above the waves. As *Kenya* passed close abeam of the silent submarine Admiral Burrough noted approvingly that Denny had brought the force across three hundred miles of open sea on a black night, the first part in very bad weather, to a position within a few hundred yards of the submarine and only one minute behind schedule. (It is typical of Captain Denny's modesty that later, in reviewing Admiral Burrough's official report on the operation, he crossed out the word "only", thus converting a commendation of himself into criticism. The regular officers of the Royal Navy are perfectionists.)

From *Tuna*'s position it was a simple compass course to the fjord mouth, skirting Klovning Island and the dangerous Skårningerne rocks to round the tip of Husevaago and the German lookout station.

Below decks, section sergeants checked ammunition loads and individual weapons. A few troopers thumbed through the Norwegian phrase books issued aboard ship, containing such useful conversation-openers as "Which way is the railroad station?" and "I love you". Captain Johnny Giles moved among his men, chatting cheerfully with everyone and watching for signs of undue nervousness. "Slinger" Martin, the administrative officer, collected twenty-four huge cans of hot cocoa from the galley and placed two in each of the landing craft hanging at the davits; there would be a long cold run-in to the beach.

High overhead the first aircraft droned in from the sea, and suddenly the action had begun.

10

SURPRISE LANDING

The same storm that raged around the surface forces as they ploughed across the North Sea towards Vaagso paid a visit to the airfields at Wick and Sumburgh, burying them in a blizzard of snow. The station operations officers received word of the twenty-four-hour postponement with considerable relief.

Throughout the 26th the winds continued to howl and more snow drifted down upon the two fields. Icicles hung from the eaves of the dispersal huts and deep snowdrifts formed on their windward side. Periodically the ground crews went out into the biting cold to sweep accumulated snow off the machines and to run up the engines lest ice form in carburettors and vapour locks in fuel lines. Late in the afternoon the storm eased up somewhat, but the wind was still bitter and occasional flurries swept the area with fresh falls of snow.

In the evening word came through that the operation was definitely "on" for the following morning. Once more the engines were run up and the fuel tanks topped off. Mechanics swept the control surfaces clear of snow and laid canvas over the perspex windscreens and warm engines. The air-crews were early to bed, for in order to adhere to the operational timetable the first sortie would have to be briefed and ready in time for a six o'clock take-off.

But as the flight crews turned in for the night and the naval elements started their final three-hundred-mile run-in the storm swept across the airfields with renewed fury. Once more snow settled on the aerodromes and the freezing winds began burnishing it into ice.

The air-crews were awakened around four, just about the same time as their commando comrades-in-arms rolled out of their bunks at sea. The sky had cleared during the last few hours but it was still as black as midnight, with a few stars beginning to show faintly through the dissipating haze. The wind had died entirely and the snowfall ceased. Sleepily the air-crews stumbled off to their mess for breakfast, while ground staff members, fortified by huge cups of hot chocolate, crunched out through the snow to ready the aircraft.

The machines with their angular outlines softened by thick mantles of snow resembled prehistoric monsters crouching in the darkness. What was worse, the snow had been packed into ice in many places.

Ground crewmen fell to with a will; wings had to be shovelled and swept clear, canopies cleaned and polished, packed snow routed out of air intakes and the hinges of control surfaces. They were still working at it, sweating by now in their heavy winter clothing and swearing furiously, when the flight crews emerged from the briefing huts and waddled out to the machines. Takeoff time was approaching, engines were already coughing and barking all up and down the line as preflight warm-ups began, and still some of the planes were partially icebound.

In the end, in order to meet the operational schedule, a few heavily-loaded aircraft staggered into the air with ice still coating parts of their wings. You want both nerve and skill for that kind of take-off.

The flight across the North Sea was uneventful. About ten miles out from the Norwegian coast they picked up the faint glimmering of the wakes of the surface elements, and as the seven ships of the "Archery" force slipped past *Tuna* and began edging up to the Husevaago lookout post the first pair of Hampdens droned in from the sea and roared over the fjord towards Rugsundo.

Fireworks erupted from Vaagso, from Maaloy and from Rugsundo.

Far below the Hampdens the throb of *Kenya*'s engines slowed as she entered the mouth of the fjord, the rest of the force falling into line astern. The towing spars were already trailing out and bow lookouts spoke muffled words into their telephones, reporting to their captains that the ships were overrunning the spar, drifting port or starboard, or holding position well. Everyone on board ship instinctively lowered his voice as they passed the tip of Husevaago, straining their eyes in search of the German outpost on the hillside above them.

It was like entering another world, going into the fjord. The ships had abandoned the open sea and seemed to be sliding deep into a tunnel hewed out of sheer rock; Brigadier Haydon felt as though by putting out both arms he could touch the fjord walls. The ships were barely maintaining steerageway in the darkness, trying to reduce the size of their bow waves which might be seen from the hillside above. Far ahead, off the starboard bow, the sheer cliffs of the Hornelen glittered faintly in the starlight.

To everyone's surprise the lighthouses at Hovdenes and Bergshomenes were burning steadily, although at reduced brilliance. (It later developed that the Germans were expecting a small coastal convoy that day, and had left the lights on.)

The weird sensation of entering that black tunnel gripped everyone, and years later many of the men who went to Vaagso would remember it more vividly than anything else about the day's events. Major Henriques, standing at his battle station on *Kenya*'s bridge, recorded his impressions:

"It was a very eerie sensation entering the fjord in absolute silence and very slowly. I wondered what was going to happen, for it seemed that the ship had lost her proper element, that she was no longer a free ship at sea. Occasionally I saw a little hut with a light burning in it and I wondered whether the light would be suddenly switched off, which would mean that the enemy had spotted us, or whether it would continue to burn as some Norwegian fisherman got out of bed, stretched himself and went off to his nets.

"As we entered the fjord the naval commander gave the order 'Hoist the battle ensign!' By tradition the navy then hauls down its normal white ensign and replaces it with a thing the size of a double sheet to give the enemy something to shoot at."

To those on board the flagship the day's action would have an entirely different character, for the Royal Navy in action has a flavour all its own. As the battle ensign was broken out a sudden calm fell over the entire ship, an air of detachment and strict politeness like that surrounding a game of croquet at the vicarage. Orderlies appeared from time to time with cups of tea or hot soup which they handed around the bridge.

Henriques and other members of the planning staff had been living aboard *Kenya* and her sister ship, H.M.S. *Nigeria,* for five weeks now, first working out the abortive assault on Floro and then preparing for the Vaagso enterprise, but no amount of shipboard living could make an army staff officer feel entirely at home. It was an entirely different world with rules of its own.

"We dined with the great," recalls Henriques, "and were squeezed into corners alongside the hammocks of the humble. I was always in the wrong place, wrongly dressed, doing the wrong thing and enjoying the freest hospitality, drinking at the expense of others, accepting their sacrifices to enhance my own comfort. All the time we were treated with a special sort of traditional kindness of such a warmth and consideration that at last we began to understand how much sea power depends upon good manners, and how the ceremonies of ordinary living build up the discipline that controls battles.

"Every now and then the ships in which we were living plunged off into the North Sea, sometimes upon their own urgent errands but more often for some purpose in which we had a share. On these occasions, however much the seas broke over our bows and inconvenienced our passage between quarter-deck and bridge, our plans and calculations had to continue. Our midnight work over charts, photographs and orders had to be carried on in the cramped and pendulous conditions to which sailors grow accustomed.

"I longed for familiar circumstances in which I had, and knew, my place. For, although most cordially accepted as partners in an enterprise, we were but strangers in a ship where sailors had a home of their own peculiar contrivance. . . . A succession of small incompatibilities made a conservative landsman feel that he and his surroundings were not concordant. Our clothes, for instance, were unsuitable and insufficient for the alternating rigours and ceremonies of the sea; our disagreeable office habits of collecting files of orders, instructions and information were frustrated by a shortage of horizontal space upon which to put them; we were always hatless at times when manners demanded that our heads be covered, while hats were inappositely in our hands when their was no obvious cranny for their concealment. We were frequently anxious to journey between decks just after the watertight doors had been secured; when we wished to sleep, loudspeakers broadcast boatswains' pipes and curious ejaculations; when we needed a clerk or a servant he was usually involved in a strangely timed repast. No word or look of reproach or mockery was ever returned to our trespass or misadventure but we could not be unconscious of our own defects."

In contrast to this period of activity and frustration, the final run across the North Sea and the entry into the fjord provided an interval of curious idleness. The last plan had been completed, the last instruction given, and everything was in its place for the opening of the battle. There was simply nothing left to do, and the army passengers found themselves resting idly while the navy worked.

Few of the army passengers had appreciated the magnitude of Captain Denny's accomplishment in bringing them straight into the target, for, as Peter Young observed, "We all had an almost touching faith in the navigational abilities of the Royal Navy—fortified by acquaintance with the career of Captain Hornblower—and did not for one moment imagine that they could not find their way anywhere, by day or night, with perfect ease."

As *Kenya* nosed into the dark fjord, a thrill of expectation ran through everyone aboard. The crew donned steel helmets; watertight doors were dogged shut. At the stern the huge battle ensign fluttered in the breeze. On the bridge, Henriques and the brigadier watched the admiral looking unconcerned as Captain Denny and the Norwegian pilot spoke quietly together, pointing from time to time at landmarks. Occasionally the Norwegian would give an order to the helmsman. Everyone watched the shoreline with fascination.

The entire "Archery" staff were at their stations. Just below the bridge, in the Flag Plot, the brigade intelligence officer, Captain Wakefield, sat with his chief clerk and two orderlies. Fastened on the table before them was a large-scale map of the target area on which they would post changes in the situation as reports came in from various elements of the raiding force. Through an eyepiece mounted on the bridge, looking down through the intervening deck by a sort of inverted-periscope arrangement, the admiral and the brigadier could examine the map without leaving their stations.

To the rear of the plot stood another separate compartment, the ship's remote-control office. Naval signallers sat ready at their sets in this room, merely monitoring their assigned wave-lengths now but ready to begin talking with other ships of the force once the action had been joined. As the cruiser entered the fjord they got into a friendly argument about whose turn it would be this time to empty the bucket at the end of the action. (When a warship goes into action and the crew are barred from the latrines by locking of the watertight doors a bucket is allotted to each compartment as a substitute facility.) Eventually they agreed to keep score and award the honour to whichever signalman used the bucket most often.

The radio sets installed in the remote-control office gave contact with home base and with other ships of the force, as well as providing a direct link with Admiral Tovey who was now manoeuvring major elements of the Home Fleet (including his flagship H.M.S. *King George V*) to amuse German naval intelligence while the "Archery" force crept into Vaagsfjord; he had little hope that the Germans might rise to the bait and send their own fleet elements out to fight, although he would have liked nothing better.

These sets were connected to the permanent aerials strung between masts and superstructure. But still more radio sets had been installed aboard *Kenya* for this voyage, for the brigadier would need to communicate with his landing force, and the R.A.F. liaison officer, a young New Zealand squadron leader, with the aircraft overhead. Army sets and operators had been crammed into every corner of the bridge, whose superstructure was now festooned with jury-rigged aerials. To go from one wing of the bridge to the other one had to tread carefully, for wires lay everywhere and there was the constant danger of tripping over a radioman muttering strange incantations into his set.

It was a lovely sight from the ships as the Hampdens swept in over the fjord and delicate trains of slowly climbing tracer rose to meet them, casting flickering shadows over the fjord. The aircraft wheeled around Rugsundo and dots of light rose to meet them as they swung around and darted back in again, almost leisurely. At first the spectacle took place in silence, but for the hum of the aircraft's engines; then the staccato popping sound of anti-aircraft weapons in the Vaagso–Maaloy area reached the ships, and at last the crump of bombs from Rugsundo.

And what of the Germans in the target area?

The schedule for Saturday morning, 27th December, called for work details to improve the defensive position south of the town, and the infantry platoon from South Vaagso was already in position for the day's work. Across the strait on little Maaloy members of the coast defence battery were seated in one of the huts listening to a lecture on military courtesy: "How to Behave in the Presence of an Officer." The battery commander, a stout, middle-aged captain named Butziger, had overslept slightly, but there was nothing demanding his immediate attention anyway; he handed his boots to an orderly for shining and wandered into the bathroom to shave.

As the British ships sailed into the dark fjord and the first Hampdens droned by overhead a sentinel at the lookout station on Husevaago peered thoughtfully down into the darkness. For just a moment he had sensed some kind of movement below him. Stepping into the nearby shed, he emerged with a pair of binoculars and raised them to his eyes. There *were* ships down there—it looked like seven blacked-out destroyers—steaming quietly past his position. He picked up a telephone and rang through to the battery command post on Maaloy.

Hauptmann Butziger was busy shaving in the adjacent room when the phone rang, but his orderly was seated at the table beside the instrument, busily shining his officer's boots. Butziger did not leave the mirror. The orderly, engrossed in working on the boots, scowled impatiently at the instrument. He bent to his work, applying the final touches of polish. Then, wiping his hands on a rag, he reached for the instrument, but as he stretched out his hand it stopped ringing.

Puzzled by the unknown warships cruising so purposefully into the fjord, the lookout on Husevaago was even more puzzled when no one answered the phone at the battery command post. He meditated briefly, then phoned the harbour captain's office in South Vaagso and reported what he had seen, but the clerk there assured him that everything was all right.

"We were expecting a small convoy this morning. Apparently they are a little ahead of schedule."

"But these did not look like merchant vessels to me," protested the lookout. "They were blacked out entirely, and looked like destroyers."

"Are you still celebrating Christmas? Take care you don't get caught drunk on your post!" The clerk in the harbour captain's office slammed down the phone and shrugged his shoulders.

But the Husevaago sentinel made one more try. He wrote a brief message on a piece of paper: 'Unidentified warships entering fjord, and handed it to the signal orderly in the shed with instructions to contact the naval signal station on Maaloy.

A signalman named Van Soest happened to be on duty at the Maaloy signal tower when this unusual message came in by blinker lamp. He flashed out an acknowledgement and then, without a thought of alerting the battery headquarters a scant hundred yards away, leapt into a rowboat and began pulling like mad across the narrow strait for the headquarters of Leutnant zur See Sebelin, the German harbourmaster.

Meanwhile, the British vessels had moved up the fjord and the two troopships, as planned, pulled off to the north side into a little inlet known as Slaaken Bay while the warships, *Kenya* in the lead, eased cautiously into position for the initial bombardment. The Germans on Rugsundo were still being tormented by the R.A.F., and the sounds of aircraft engines and distant gunfire nearly drowned out the muted command from loudspeakers on *Prince Leopold* and *Prince Charles:* "Lower boats to embarkation level."

Quickly and efficiently the raiding force filed up from below deck and manned the dangling Higgins boats, and at exactly 0839 all the landing craft hit the water simultaneously amid a rattle of chains and creaking of blocks. A few of the boats had brief difficulty in unhooking from the falls but then the blocks fell clear and with a quiet purr of engines the tiny craft sorted themselves out into the designated columnar formation. At 0842, one minute behind schedule, the little flotilla churned away from the mother ships and faded into the darkness.

They were in two columns, boats from *Prince Charles* on the port (north) side and boats from *Prince Leopold* on the starboard (south). The last two A.L.C.s from *Leopold*, carrying Clement's 2 Troop, soon broke off from the column and ran directly in towards shore; the column was already abreast of their landing point among the rocks near Hollevik, and they were to be first to land.

Durnford-Slater was in the leading A.L.C. of the port column with a load of commandos and Lieutenant N. P. C. Hastings, R.N.V.R., *Prince Charles*'s boat officer. He clutched a Verey pistol in his hand and nine more lay within reach; the signal to lift the bombardment would be ten Verey flares and he had decided that reloading nine times took up too much time.

Just to the left of the column rode a support landing craft (S.L.C.), a modified A.L.C. mounting a mortar and two machine guns suitable for use in either an anti-aircraft or ground support role. This unusual craft could support the attack as needed from any point along the shoreline, as it also carried extra armour-plating to protect the crew. It was a commando innovation.

Off to their right in the deeper waters of the fjord the commando soldiers in the boats could see *Kenya*, with *Onslow* tight on her starboard beam and *Offa* almost welded to her stern, nosing ahead to her designated position opposite Maaloy.

The starboard column carried the troops bound for Maaloy, and they were crouched low in their boats as they approached the corner of land which would expose them to the German battery. *Kenya* and the two destroyers glided ahead in complete silence. The first faint glimmering of dawn began to appear in the sky.

As the warships coasted slowly around the point Maaloy came into view from the cruiser's bridge; dimly seen in the still waters of the fjord, it resembled merely a pale swelling jutting above the surface of the water.

Then Admiral Burrough glanced at his watch and spoke five words.

"Open the line of fire."

The bridge talker repeated the order to fire control and *Kenya*'s guns exploded into life with a blinding flash. A moment

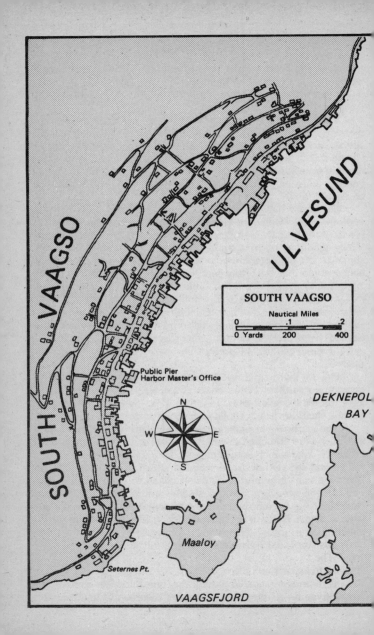

SOUTH VAAGSO

SOUTH VAAGSO

Nautical Miles

0   .1   .2

0 Yards   200   400

ULVESUND

DEKNEPOL
BAY

Public Pier
Harbor Master's Office

N
W   E
S

Maaloy

Seternes Pt.

VAAGSFJORD

later, as the first salvo of star shell hung in the air and *Kenya*'s guns began spewing out high explosive, a flash and a roar from the starboard bow announced that *Onslow* was in firing position and had joined in.

The German naval signaller, Van Soest, had already reached the pier at South Vaagso. Hastily securing his rowboat to a piling, he dashed up to the Hagen Hotel, where Leutnant zur See Sebelin had his headquarters. He reported to Sebelin and handed him the message from the Husevaago lookout station. Sebelin read it and immediately asked whether Van Soest had notified the battery headquarters on Maaloy of the contents of the message. The abashed signalman could only stammer, "No, sir. After all, they are an army battery and this is a naval signal!"

At that moment the windows rattled from the shock of a thunderous explosion somewhere nearby. An instant later a series of loud pops followed and a string of flares hung in the sky over Maaloy; it was the first star shell salvo from *Kenya*, signalling the opening of the battle. Sebelin and Van Soest stared in shocked surprise at the dazzling glare shining into the room. Then there was another crash and Maaloy Island dissolved in smoke and flame as the first salvo of high explosives tore into the battery positions. The time was 0848.

Kenya poured one broadside after another into the tiny island, smothering it with six-inch shells. *Onslow* had pulled ahead on *Kenya*'s disengaged side and joined in, and as the two warships continued to slide slowly forward, hurling shells as fast as their crews could reload, *Offa* rounded the point behind *Kenya* and opened up.

Too late now for any German gunner in the barracks on Maaloy to run for his gun. Nothing could live in the open on the island, so heavily was it being pounded.

The German infantry working around their prepared defence positions south of the town gaped in astonishment. For just a moment they were paralysed by shock, and watched helplessly as the shells rained on the Maaloy battery only a few hundred yards away. Then they jumped for their holes; a column of landing craft could clearly be seen moving across their front towards the battery's position.

The two columns of landing craft had by now separated and turned towards their respective landing points. Maaloy was still taking a beating as the three warships hurled a rain of high explosives on to the island. It was "saturation gunnery" at its most deadly: between four and five hundred six-inch shells fell into an area less than 250 yards square in nine minutes.

In the distance the Hampdens were still buzzing angrily around the Rugsundo battery. There were a few more of them now, but the newcomers were merely putting on a show for the Germans' benefit; crammed into their bomb bays were the smoke floats for the landing points and as they circled west of Rugsundo the pilots kept their eyes turned towards Vaagso, watching for Durnford-Slater's flares to signal the start of their bomb run.

Under cover of all the noise and confusion, Clement and 2 Troop were already ashore at Hollevik, and now the other boats were less than two hundred yards from their landing points. *Offa* shifted her fire from Maaloy to the German strongpoint south of the town, where a machine-gun had begun to chatter at the approaching landing craft.

Durnford-Slater glanced over towards the other column, Jack Churchill's group. The timing was near-perfect. Both groups would ground at just about the same moment. He raised the first Verey pistol and reached out for the second. Churchill's boats were almost up to the beach—barely a hundred yards to go. He squeezed the trigger and the first flare arced into the sky, and the second. Before he could fire the third the first of ten similar flares rose from *Kenya*'s bridge and the bombardment ceased as suddenly as it had begun.

Maaloy lay hidden under a pall of smoke.

In the sudden silence, as the echoes of the last high explosive rounds died away and twenty red Verey flares fell sizzling into the water, the watchers on *Kenya*'s bridge became aware of several sounds: the growl of the landing craft making their final dash for the shore; the chatter of a machine-gun above the South Vaagso landing point; a few sharp pops faintly heard from the direction of Hollevik; and then the swelling roar of a section of Hampdens boring in at low level to mask the landing points with smoke floats.

11

BATTLE OF MAALOY

Jack Churchill's Group III consisted of Captain Ronald's 5 Troop and Captain Young's 6 Troop, and as the landing craft fanned out into a line of four boats abreast, Young's men, whose mission was to take out the three left guns of the German battery, were on the left and Ronald's, who would clear the landing place, get the fourth gun and sweep up the longer eastern side of the island, on the right.

Churchill had chosen to ride into battle with 6 Troop. Once the preliminary bombardment began and further silence became unnecessary if not superfluous he unlimbered his treasured bagpipe and began happily honking "The March of the Cameron Men". The non-highlanders, who were by far the majority faction in the troop, affected to wince at some of the louder squeals and groans emanating from the instrument, but even they found themselves strangely stirred by the old martial music; wags who claim that Scottish troops advance so bravely simply because they are trying to get away from the racket of the unit's pipers overlook the tingling response it sets up in the blood.

On the opposite side of the boat Peter Young stood erect, peering over the ramp and giving a running commentary on the scene ahead. From time to time one or another of the men would bob up to have a look for himself, only to be ordered curtly to get down. There were a lot of dry mouths at first, but as the boats drew closer to the shore the apprehension melted away and was replaced by a more sanguinary mood. This was action at last!

After two tempestuous nights at sea the waters of the fjord seemed smooth as a millpond, rippled only by the concussion of the naval guns pounding Maaloy. The island was a chaos of smoke, flame, explosions and flying debris. The prominent German signal tower had already disappeared, knocked flat by

Handley-Page Hampton

the bombardment; wooden huts, faintly seen through the mist and smoke, shuddered and collapsed. British eyes strained to see into the inferno but it was impossible to see the German defences.

Then far off to the left Durnford-Slater's Verey flares hung in the air and the bombardment stopped as suddenly as it had begun. There was a drone of engines and the men in the boats could see the oddly-shaped Hampdens skimming in like immense dragonflies; seen from the landing craft the machines seemed to be barely floating over the water but in point of fact they were thundering in on the landing point at fifty feet actual and better than two hundred knots. The Hampdens zoomed away and the smoke bombs aimed at the Maaloy landing point landed smack on target. A moment later the landing craft grounded and ramps slapped down on to the shore.

Jack Churchill turned aside to stow his bagpipe safely out of the way and as he did so Peter Young brushed by him and darted ashore. 5 and 6 Troops both swarmed out of their landing craft without a shot being fired at them. Surprise seemed completely on their side.

Directly in front of the boats was a short but steep rocky slope. The men scrambled up to the top and paused momentarily to deploy into line for the assault. During this brief pause Major Churchill took the lead again; brandishing his sword and shouting hoarsely, he bolted through the astonished commandos and vanished into the smoke. The leading elements took a deep breath and plunged after him, but they would not catch up or even see him again until the battle had ended on Maaloy.

It was impossible to see more than a few yards in the dense smoke around the landing place, and as they began to move forward from the landing area 5 and 6 Troops lost contact, operating completely independently of one another for the rest of the action.

The first combat task had been assigned to 5 Troop: clear the landing area of any German resistance. The aerial photographs had pinpointed a German machine-gun position on the right flank of the beach, and according to plan a subsection rushed off into the smoke to find it. At that moment three German soldiers were sitting behind the gun, stunned and confused by the shelling they had undergone and completely blinded by the dense smoke which concealed the Englishmen debarking a scant hundred yards away.

Despite the limited visibility the 5 Troop assault squad's sense of direction was true and when they burst out the other side of the smoke cloud the gun was right in front of them, scarcely ten yards away. Before the three startled gunners could react Private Grigg had killed two of them with a single burst from his sub-machine-gun. The third German immediately threw up his hands and was taken prisoner. The machine-gun had not fired a shot and the main threat to the landing beach had been eliminated.

6 Troop was already well into the German battery position. On the extreme left Lieutenant R. J. Wills's section was scrambling up the slope near the westernmost point of the island, aiming for the left two guns of the battery. The smoke cloud here was so dense that Wills decided to take his men around rather than through it. Before going very far they stumbled into a barbed wire entanglement, but it had not been prepared in any depth and was easily breached. Pushing on, they suddenly came upon the first of the guns, sitting alone and undefended in its emplacement. Wills and a few men darted off to the left and found the other gun; cautiously approaching it, they found this position too completely undefended. They tumbled into the gun pit and paused to catch their breath and puzzle over the lack of enemy resistance; it was completely unexpected that their seizure of the guns should go unchallenged.

6 Troop's other section had pushed straight inland from the landing point, aiming for the battery's number three gun and the barracks behind it. Captain Young was with this section since Lieutenant Brandwood, the section officer, had been told off to command the demolition squads on the island. Almost immediately after clearing the cliff top Young's men floundered into some barbed wire, lying uprooted after the naval bombardment.

It is one of the basic rules of the military profession that one always sites automatic weapons to cover one's wire entanglements, for wire alone cannot delay an attacker for long; Young was puzzled that they should be walking right through the barricades without drawing fire. Where the devil were the Germans?

The smoke inside the barrier was still thick. Suddenly the parapet of the gun position loomed ahead. The commandos crept close, then dashed the few remaining yards and vaulted over the wall, but still there were no Germans to be seen. The battered gun stood alone.

5 Troop's left section had taken the fourth gun at the same time, finding it similarly undefended. Eight minutes had passed since the boats grounded at the landing point, all four guns of the German battery had been seized without incident, and thus far only three German soldiers had been encountered on the whole island; yet a lot more of them were somewhere around, no one knew where. The suspense was terrific. Dropping off a few men to guard the captured guns, the commandos began redeploying for an advance towards the remaining objectives.

Looking down the back side of the hill they could see the German barracks; many of the buildings were ablaze. Not an enemy soldier could be seen.

Suddenly a lone German bolted out of one of the barracks buildings and charged straight towards the commandos crouching in the number three gun position. Lance-Sergeant Herbert, off to the right with his subsection, saw him come out the door and tried to snap off a quick shot but his rifle misfired. Then Captain Young, Sergeant Vincent and one of the Norwegian soldiers saw him and they all fired, nearly simultaneously. The German let out a choked scream and collapsed. Somewhere off to the right a grenade exploded.

The shooting of this one German broke the tension that had been building up steadily since the British first stepped ashore. Captain Young just had time to mutter, "Well, if I'm killed today I'll be taking at least one of them with me," and then things began to happen.

The grenade explosion on the right had signalled another minor enemy contact. Sergeant Connolly, advancing with his subsection along the right margin of 6 Troop's assigned sector, spotted two Germans peering out of a small wooden hut. He pointed them out to a trooper named Durling who happened to have a grenade in his hand and yelled to everyone to duck.

Durling let fly with the grenade and everyone, including the two Germans, hit the ground—except a slightly deaf commando named Walsh who failed to hear his sergeant's warning and darted forward just in time to get a nasty but non-critical wound from a fragment which pierced his neck. The two Germans surrendered and the bleeding Walsh marched them back to the beach.

Sergeant Herbert was puzzling over the single German who had come out of the barracks and run straight towards the British. The man's behaviour seemed irrational; what had he been trying to do? Certainly a one-man counterattack seemed unlikely.

Then the answer dawned. The man must have been running for some type of shelter, unaware that the British troops were on the island. That would explain the lack of resistance: the Germans were in their air raid shelters and still did not know that anything more than an air attack had taken place! Herbert called out to the rest of his section to cover him, and moved out into the open to find a vantage point from whence he might locate the shelters.

Directly below him, masked by the curve of the hill, he found a small hut, just about on the path the dead German had been taking when shot. He ran down and peered cautiously around the edge of the door. The room inside the hut ran some distance back into the hillside, and was filled with German soldiers. He had stumbled across the battery's main air raid shelter.

Herbert stepped back and pulled the pin on a grenade but just as he drew his arm back to bowl it in the door a cheerful voice called out, "It's all right, George, we've got the bastards."

Unobserved by Sergeant Herbert, Lance-Corporal Hall and Trooper Hughes had come around the other end of the hut and now they took position at the opposite entrance, flourishing their sub-machine-guns at the startled Germans who promptly began filing out with their hands above their heads.

The shelter yielded about fifteen prisoners, among them the hapless Butziger. Their capture solved the mystery of the lack of resistance on the island, and the British began to poke carefully into anything that looked as if it might offer shelter from an air attack.

5 Troop on the right was pushing up the shank of the island, meeting with no further opposition. A few startled Germans were

flushed out of dugouts and from under sheds; most of them were suffering the effects of shock as a consequence of the violent bombardment they had had to endure. Ronald's men turned to the task of searching the enemy positions for documents and destroying the few installations of value left intact by the naval gunners.

Lieutenant Wills had left a few men behind to guard the captured German guns and was hurrying down the reverse slope of the hill with the rest of his section, guiding on the blazing barracks and storage sheds on the northern shore. They almost tripped over a horribly mutilated German writhing in agony on the ground. The man had been caught in the open by the beginning of the bombardment and was obviously beyond any hope of recovery. After a moment of sick hesitation while the dying soldier moaned and jerked one of the Englishmen fired a single shot and they went on.

A German patrol boat in the harbour north of the island spotted them edging up to the buildings as they emerged from the protection of a small patch of woods, and fired a long burst. Several of Wills's men fired back but the boat was beyond rifle range and moving away; the German fire died away as a trooper and a lance-corporal burst into the first building, which proved to be unoccupied. Weapons at the ready, they combed the remaining structures and emerged with two prisoners—a German soldier and a terrified "comfort girl" who passed her time on the island entertaining the enemy troops.

Captain Young and Lance-Corporal Harper wandered into the complex of burning buildings, looking for the battery headquarters; other parties of British were poking about among the ruins, looking for hidden Germans. As they rounded a corner, Young suddenly found himself face-to-face with two armed German soldiers who were just as startled as he was. He sprang back around the corner and turned to Harper.

"There are two of them there," he said. "We'll go around the corner together."

Young raised his bayonet-tipped rifle and Harper his tommy gun. With a sudden shout of *"Hande hoch!"* they jumped into view. The nearer German's reaction was completely unexpected—he grabbed for Young's bayonet and tried to disarm him.

Young snatched his rifle back out of the German's reach but at that moment the enemy soldier lost his nerve; he whirled and tried to run. Young lowered his rifle again and snapped off a shot

and the German staggered. The second man raised his pistol and
Harper cut loose with his tommy gun. Trooper Clark, skidding
around the corner behind Young and Harper at that moment,
fired his rifle without taking time to aim. The three commandos
dodged back around the corner, someone threw a grenade over
the roof, and when the smoke cleared the two Germans lay dead
on the ground.

Lieutenant Brandwood's demolition party found two more
Germans hiding under the adjacent building. They were so
terrified that Brandwood could not persuade them to emerge. At
length Private "Curly" Gimbert, a big, good-natured man with
the build of a medieval blacksmith, crawled under the building
and dragged them out by the ankles. The two prisoners proved to
be sailors, dressed neatly but not warmly in thin naval uniforms
with white trousers. They wore steel helmets but were unarmed.
Captain Young, who happened by just then, actually felt sorry
for them. They looked miserable and out of place in the middle
of an infantry engagement.

At 0920 Major Churchill sent a signal to the flagship,
reporting that all objectives had been secured and the entire
island overrun. The battle of Maaloy, foreseen as the toughest
part of the day's action, had turned out to be the easiest. It was
over in less than twenty minutes and for all practical purposes
had been won in the first eight when the major objective—the
capture of the German guns and neutralization of the battery—
had been attained. Careful planning and preparation, accurate
gunnery and sheer luck (for how else may one explain the
German orderly's failure to answer the telephone?) had turned
what could well have been a bloody and difficult assault into a
simple walkover.

From the harbour north of the island the British soldiers
were in plain sight as they poked about among the rocks looking
for Germans. The armed trawler north of the island opened fire
again.

The number 2 gun of the German battery was still in good
working order, so Troopers Mapplebeck and Hannan of 6 Troop
swung it around to point north and took the trawler under fire.
Hannan laid the gun and Mapplebeck loaded. Neither was a
trained gunner or knew anything much about artillery, but the
trawler was an easy target, being just 900 yards away, so
eventually they began to score some hits. Unfortunately they
knew nothing about fuse-setting so none of the rounds burst upon

impact. At that moment Sergeant Vincent, who had been a
gunner before joining 3 Commando, happened along on his
mission of setting charges to destroy the breechblocks of the
weapons; he offered to set the fuses but Jack Churchill had seen
the ineffective fire Hannan and Mapplebeck were putting out and
sent up word to cease fire and stop making so bloody much noise
so he could think about getting on with the war.

Brigadier Haydon acknowledged Churchill's report of the
battery's capture and instructed him to send off a force to blow
up the Mortenes herring oil factory at Deknepol on the far side of
the fjord. This mission was assigned to 5 Troop, so Captain
Ronald loaded about half his men on one of the assault landing
craft and off they went. No one really expected any Germans to
be around the factory—the intelligence folder had been specific
about that—but there was not much point in being half-safe so
they were prepared for the worst when they left; the A.L.C.
fairly bristled with weapons.

The folder was correct. Ronald and his detachment found
no one at the factory but a Norwegian watchman, who gave no
argument and moved off to a safe distance when told what was
going to happen. Shortly after the boat grounded at Deknepol,
the factory shuddered and then collapsed with a muffled boom,
the wreckage hanging out over the water. Ronald loaded his men
back on the landing craft for the return trip.

12

GROUP I ADVANCES

Although Maaloy with its German battery was a more important objective, the first British troops to land had actually gone ashore at Hollevik to deal with the reported field gun on the hill behind the village.

Lieutenant Clement's Group I consisted of his own understrength 2 Troop (3 officers and 43 other ranks) plus a 4-man *Kompani Linge* detachment under Lieutenant Harold Risnes, Norwegian Army. They landed in two A.L.C.s, on the left Clement with Lieutenant John Chatton's section and on the right Risnes with the section commanded by Lieutenant Denis O'Flaherty.

The two section officers made a strange contrast. Chatton, a grey-haired old regular, was one of the oldest men in 3 Commando, being almost a contemporary of "Slinger" Martin. Formerly a regimental sergeant-major, he had been awarded a wartime commission and soon found his way into the commandos. O'Flaherty was a young regular officer of the Royal Artillery whose term at Woolwich had been cut short by the war. An energetic young fire-eater, surreptitiously known among the other ranks as "Lieutenant O'Flighty", O'Flaherty was a new-comer to 2 Troop. Just before the raid he had been detached from Captain Giles's 3 Troop to attend a signals course; during his absence Giles's younger brother, Lieutenant Bruce Giles, joined 3 Commando and O'Flaherty was shifted to 2 Troop so that the brothers might serve together.

2 Troop's landing point was marked by a prominent house some twenty yards from the shore, facing on to the coastal road with its back towards the water. The supposed German gun position was on the hillside directly above. As the boats moved in towards the shore at the first moment of dawn, Clement squinted at the icy hill rising some two hundred feet above the

fjord. The slope appeared to be about sixty degrees and would offer tough footing.

The right-hand boat touched ground first, banging solidly home against a group of protruding rocks below the houses of Hollevik. O'Flaherty and Risnes were first out. They climbed quickly to the level of the coastal road, the rest of their men stringing out behind them, passed to the right of the house and stepped out on to the road.

From somewhere behind them a shot rang out; it seemed to have come from the house. They could see Clement and Chatton coming up the slope on their left with the other section, still between the house and the sea, so Risnes and O'Flaherty turned and went straight for the front door. It was locked.

Risnes hammered on the door and shouted in Norwegian for the occupants to open up, meanwhile trying to restrain O'Flaherty who was doing his best to kick the door in. There was no response so Risnes stepped aside and O'Flaherty shot the lock out with his .45 pistol. Bursting in the door, they caught a quick glimpse of two Germans in blue uniforms and black helmets scurrying down a short flight of steps to the back door. O'Flaherty fired and nicked one of them in the backside as he went out of the door but Lance-Corporal Gittens who was waiting outside with a sub-machine-gun spotted them as they emerged and dropped them with two quick bursts. The critically wounded Germans were carried aboard one of the landing craft and evacuated immediately to *Prince Leopold* for treatment.

Meanwhile, Lieutenant Risnes found a civilian hiding in the house and questioned him at some length while O'Flaherty started up the hill towards the gun position with his section. The man denied that there was any German gun on the hill or anywhere else in the near vicinity. The two wounded Germans had been members of a ten-man marine guard detachment; the other eight had walked into South Vaagso for breakfast an hour earlier and had not yet returned.

Risnes went out on to the road and shouted up to O'Flaherty, who was by this time almost into the suspected gun position, that the position was unoccupied. O'Flaherty confirmed this in a moment and started back down the hill.

Clement tried to radio a report to the colonel, who by this time was ashore in South Vaagso, but he could not make contact. So he sent the message instead to Brigadier Haydon on the flagship. The brigadier relayed the message to Durnford-Slater

Me 109

and instructed Clement to move his troop up the coastal road according to plan and come into reserve for Group II in South Vaagso.

Clement instructed O'Flaherty to lead off with his section and O'Flaherty set off at a fast pace, alert for any sign of the rest of the enemy marine detachment returning down the coastal road.

In a few minutes O'Flaherty's section spotted another blue-clad figure ahead and bellowed at him to stand fast and hold his hands above his head. Instead, the man bolted into a notch in the cliff beside the road and disappeared. A Mills bomb soon fetched him out, sick with fear and stunned by the detonation but otherwise unhurt. To the disgust of the landing party, he turned out to be a civilian in a peaked cap and not a German as they had thought.

It was broad daylight by now, somewhere around ten o'clock in the morning. Overhead an R.A.F. Blenheim fighter circled watchfully, and from ahead they could hear a continuous rattle of small arms fire punctuated by bursting grenades. As they neared the town an Me–109 suddenly flashed past, skimming over the waters of the fjord on a course paralleling the coastal road and barely fifty feet away; with a little advance warning any of them could have hit it with a rock. Everyone let fly with rifles, tommy guns and Brens but the aircraft was already out of range. It bored straight ahead for a few moments, then suddenly zoomed almost straight up and climbed underneath the tail of the patrolling Blenheim high above. The Blenheim's blind spots were no mystery to the Germans, for they had captured several specimens intact when France fell and test-flown them to their heart's content. O'Flaherty and his men watched in horror while the Messerschmitt moved leisurely into position directly under the Blenheim's tail and then shot it to pieces. The British pilot never knew what hit him.

Near Group II's landing point they met Captain Corry, 3 Commando's Irish doctor. He was fuming about the Messerschmitt too, not so much because it had shot down the Blenheim but because just before pulling up it had idly sprayed his aid station with machine-gun bullets. Fortunately no one had been hit.

At the first corner in South Vaagso O'Flaherty ran into Alan Smallman, the adjutant. Only when Smallman asked him where the rest of 2 Troop was did O'Flaherty realize that Clement and Chatton were no longer behind him. He set about signalling back down the road by wigwag and lamp but could see no response so finally in disgust he trotted back in search of Clement.

The reason for the delay was logical enough; Clement was exercising his own initiative to check on a peculiar phenomenon he had observed from shipboard when the first Hampdens flew in over the fjord. A stream of tracers had seemed to rise right out of the larger hill behind the one where the German gun had been reported. Was their an anti-aircraft gun on the higher hill? Clement decided to delay in Halnoesvik long enough for Chatton's section to check the higher hill.

Chatton had just returned with a negative report[1] when the puffing O'Flaherty galloped around the last turn in the road,

---

[1]There was not in fact any gun on the hill. The illusion of tracers coming from the hilltop was probably caused by seeing fire from the German guns in and around South Vaagso, directly over the hill, firing almost straight up into the air.

yelled to get their attention, made the ''follow me'' sign, and led
off again towards South Vaagso.

When he got back to the command post in South Vaagso
O'Flaherty found Charley Head momentarily in charge while the
colonel had a look at things up forward. The battle was not going
well in the town and reinforcements were needed. Without
waiting for Clement to catch up, O'Flaherty went forward with
his own men.

When Clement arrived a few minutes later with the balance
of the troop, he was given little more information. 3 and 4
Troops had caught a tartar in South Vaagso, casualties were
running high, and the attack had stalled. 2 Troop was to pitch in
immediately, move from south to north through the town, and try
to get things moving again. O'Flaherty had crossed over to the
right of the coastal road to back up 4 Troop; Clement and the
others would push forward in the western half of the town,
through 3 Troop's assigned sector.

13

BATTLE THROUGH THE STREETS

As Durnford-Slater pointed his second Verey pistol skyward and
pressed the trigger the boat officer, Lieutenant Hastings, gave the
''Blue turn'' signal and the entire column of Higgins boats
pivoted sharply and swung in towards the Group II landing
place, a jumble of rocks at the base of a near-vertical cliff rising
some thirty feet to the level of the coastal road. Just as the
colonel's boat grounded the first of the Hampdens roared in
overhead and laid its parachute-stabilized smoke bomb neatly on
the cliff edge, from tree-top height. So close was the explosion
that as Durnford-Slater leapt ashore tiny bits of burning phosphorus spattered on his sleeves, setting the outer layer of clothing
afire. He beat the flames out with his gloves and brushed away
the particles before they could burn through to his skin.

The armed German trawler *Föhn*, lying in the Ulvesund just

north of Maaloy, put a burst squarely into the second Hampden
as it swept across the island towards the South Vaagso landing
point; one engine immediately began to stream smoke. The pilot,
a cool and determined flight sergeant named Smith, held steady
on his course, fighting to keep the damaged aircraft level.
Despite Smith's best efforts the aircraft gradually fell off on one
wing as it approached the bomb release point; under the circumstances the bombardier was unable to make a precision drop and
let the smoke bomb go just a moment too soon, right over the
assault craft as they neared the shore.

Lieutenant Arthur Komrower, riding into battle with his
section of Forrester's 4 Troop, glanced up and saw the bomb
swaying under its parachute; although the odds against such a
thing were fantastic, it was coming right into the boat. Komrower
shouted out a warning and hurled himself over one corner of the
bow ramp into the sea. The bomb settled squarely into the
middle of the landing craft and ignited among the closely-packed
troops. Men and equipment were sprayed with phosphorus and
burning oil. Several soldiers were killed outright and most of the
rest badly burned, some of them fatally. A second later the boat
grounded on a rock at the landing point and the injured coxswain
quickly dropped the ramp. The ammunition on board had ignited
and bullets and flares began to spray in all directions as the
survivors staggered ashore, dragging their wounded with them.

"Slinger" Martin was sitting atop a great pile of reserve
ammunition in the boat immediately behind. "A tremendous
fountain of flame and sparks, like a Roman candle" surged into
the air, and pieces of burning phosphorus pattered into Martin's
boat. Some of them landed on the ammunition. He and his men
managed to keep the flames from igniting the high explosive, but
a radio set carried by the Headquarters Signals Section in the
forward part of the boat caught fire and blazed up so fiercely that
they finally had to push it overboard.

Lieutenant Komrower's wild dive over the corner of the
ramp had saved him from the effects of the explosion, but when
the boat grounded on the rocks a moment later his leg was
crushed, pinning him helplessly in place. He struggled weakly to
free himself as the ammunition in the boat began exploding and
the boat burned hotly. Martin Linge spotted Komrower's plight
and splashed into the water beside him. Disregarding the dangers
of exploding ammunition and choking in the oily white smoke
pouring from the disabled craft, Linge began rocking the boat

back and forth until suddenly Komrower's leg pulled free and he was able to crawl to safety. Then Linge charged off into the smoke which completely obscured the town from the landing point.

Apart from the casualties in this one boat Group II had managed to get ashore intact. A few bursts of fire from the German strongpoint crackled over their heads during the final moments of the run-in but no harm was done and then the low cliff sheltered them from the enemy. In less than a minute the first men of 3 and 4 Troops were emerging atop the cliff, where burning phosphorus still flamed in tiny crevasses. Dense white smoke obscured the landing area; bullets cracked and snapped as the Germans manning the strongpoint fired blindly into the oily vapour. Lieutenant Lloyd had barely reached the top of the cliff with a few of his men when they "bush-whacked" (to use Lloyd's Australian term) a group of Germans galloping down the coastal road towards their positions just south of the town. Captain Giles bellowed "Come on!" and disappeared into the smoke with 3 Troop at his heels, moving straight ahead towards the strongpoint. Captain Forrester, momentarily puzzled, looked around the clifftop and then suddenly realized that the missing elements of his troop must have been on board the landing craft hit by the bomb; he waved his arm and plunged into the smoke on Giles's right, steering 4 Troop up the right-hand sector of the town, closest to the waterfront.

At the base of the cliff Doctor Corry was tending the casualties from Komrower's flaming craft while "Slinger" Martin and his storesmen unloaded ammunition from their own. A human chain moved the crates and sacks rapidly up the cliff to the roadside. The burning landing craft, still blazing and crackling with exploding ammunition, was finally pushed out into the fjord to drift away on the current. It sank a short distance from the shore and was later salvaged by the Germans.

Meanwhile, Captain Bradley had moved his 1 Troop up the cliff behind 3 and 4 Troops to start sorting out its various tasks. These included securing the landing area, locating and destroying an anti-aircraft gun reported near the south-west corner of the town (actually a part of the German strongpoint with which 3 Troop was already engaged), and carrying out the main demolition tasks as the two assault troops uncovered targets. In addition, Bradley's troop was to be prepared to lend a hand anywhere the attack might run into trouble. Bradley had

3″ Mortar

somehow scrounged up a three-inch mortar and on his own initiative had organized a mortar detachment to man it during the Vaagso raid, an innovation in the Commando organization but one he felt might on the whole prove useful.

The battle in the streets of South Vaagso was by far the fiercest and bloodiest part of the day's fighting, for here, rather than an artillery battery cowering in air raid shelters, the commandos encountered an alert group of German combat soldiers, well armed, well led and skilled at house-to-house fighting. Most of these men were veterans of the 1940 Norwegian campaign, and they met the British head-on. During the first commando assault on the strongpoint the infantry platoon leader, Oberleutnant

Bremer, was killed. So was the unit's chaplain; other Germans fell around him. Command of the German forces in this critical area soon devolved upon the senior non-commissioned officer, Stabsfeldwebel Lebrenz, a tough veteran of the 1940 campaign. In the town itself the German harbourmaster, Sebelin, improvised a second defensive line using headquarters troops, sailors, and any other German he could lay hands on. The battle soon resolved itself into a series of isolated skirmishes in which groups of determined men burst open the doors of buildings from which equally determined snipers challenged their advance, organized room-to-room assaults, and ran slipping and stumbling through bleak alleys and snow-covered backyards to roll over board fences into the adjacent yards while bullets threw up little sprays of snow at their feet. It was the most brutal type of fighting; neither side asked for quarter and neither side was much inclined to give it. While the battle raged Norwegian families cowered in their cellars, wincing at the crack of bullets and crash of breaking glass above their heads.

Casualties mounted quickly on both sides. Chance encounters at corners led to sudden bursts of automatic weapons fire; subsection and squad leaders shouted hasty commands in English and German; then no sound was left but the groans of the wounded as the fighting moved up the street.

Less than fifteen minutes after landing, 3 Troop ran into a major obstacle to its advance. German infantrymen firing from the windows of a large Norwegian home stood firmly in the troop's path and would not be dislodged. Slowly and skilfully the British worked their way closer to the building, killing three of the enemy in the process. Finally Captain Giles himself led a wild charge and burst in through the front door. They went from room to room, throwing open doors and rolling grenades inside. At last the surviving Germans fled out the back door but as Giles stepped into the doorway behind them a German lying in the garden shot him through the stomach. He died within seconds.

At just about the same time the troop's senior subaltern, Lieutenant Mike Hall, was hit by a German bullet which shattered his left elbow, and two more men were killed evacuating him under fire. The mantle of command now fell upon Lieutenant Bruce Giles. Giles did his best to keep the attack going, but he was in a state of shock after seeing his idolized older brother cut down before his eyes; his heart was no longer in it. German resistance was stiffening as the enemy troops recovered from their initial surprise and steadied under fire. 3 Troop's assault gradually ground to a halt.

4 Troop on the right was having little better fortune. Almost immediately after leaving the landing point Bill Lloyd went down with a bullet through his neck. He was sent to the rear, bleeding copiously and furious with disappointment. Lieutenant Komrower hobbled forward on an improvised cane, trying to catch up with his own section; he was still determined to get into action. Captain Forrester kept the whole troop moving by himself, going straight up the main street, whooping and shouting to encourage his men. Durnford-Slater caught a brief glimpse of him, "throwing grenades into each house as he came to it and firing from the hip with his tommy gun. He looked wild and dangerous. I shouldn't have liked to have been a German in his path."

Hot on the heels of their commander, 4 Troop fought through to the centre of the town. The Germans under Lieutenant Sebelin had established an improvised defensive position around the Ulvesund Hotel. Forrester led a frontal assault on the building and was just about to throw a grenade through the open front door when one of the Germans inside shot him. He fell forward on top of his own grenade, which exploded a moment later.

The only officer still alive on the scene was Martin Linge, who had been pushing forward through 4 Troop's sector with two companions, trying to reach the German headquarters before any secret documents could be destroyed. Most of the British soldiers knew and respected Linge, so now he took command of 4 Troop and led another assault on the hotel. As he charged around the corner of the adjacent building two bullets pierced his chest; he stumbled forward and fell almost across the doorstep of the hotel. The attackers withdrew again.

It was known that the Germans kept a tank in the town, the old relic captured in France in 1940. It was customarily housed in the small garage adjacent to the hotel and now as the attack ebbed from the hotel itself a two-man demolition team from 1 Troop arrived to deal with the tank.

The vehicle belonged to the infantry security platoon quartered in the town but apparently the man responsible for operating it must have been caught in the first assault on the strongpoint, for no one had moved it from the garage. Sergeant Cork and Trooper Dowling ducked into the building and found it standing there, innocently awaiting its end. The momentum of Captain

Forrester's last attack had swept the Germans away from the garage and Cork and Dowling had a clear field. They set charges all the way around the tank and as Dowling crawled out the door Cork lit the fuses. A moment later the garage blew apart with a deafening explosion, killing Cork. Pieces of rubble, some of them as big as a football, whizzed down the street. Dowling was miraculously uninjured, but men two hundred yards away were hurt by flying debris.

Napoleon once remarked that every soldier carries a field-marshal's baton in his knapsack. Now as 4 Troop lay stunned and leaderless the baton emerged from an unlikely knapsack indeed: Corporal "Knocker" White, one of those soldiers who give their superiors ulcers in peacetime but are a joy to command in action when the enemy is at hand, watched the attack lose its momentum and gradually peter out as the officers fell before the German positions. Not even a sergeant was left on his feet within White's range of vision and the hated Germans seemed to be getting the best of the encounter. Taking a deep breath, White stood up and began giving orders—tentatively at first, then with growing assurance as he saw them obeyed. The transformation was amazing; the surviving members of 4 Troop reloaded their weapons, grouped around White, and then went at the Germans with renewed fury. At this critical moment Sergeant Ramsey appeared with the 1 Troop mortar detachment and lobbed ten rounds through the roof of the hotel. White and his men, accompanied by the two vengeful *Kompani Linge* soldiers who had seen their captain die, threw a shower of grenades into exposed doors and windows and charged. 4 Troop's attack overran the blazing building at last.

The colonel had come forward to find out why the attack was moving so slowly. Now he ordered Captain Bradley to bring up every man who could be spared from 1 Troop's principal tasks; he himself would go back to the headquarters and try to arrange for more reinforcements in the meantime.

By the time he got back to his headquarters group and the radios, Brigadier Haydon was calling for him: could Group II make use of the reserve troop? Maaloy had already fallen and apparently the reserve would not be needed elsewhere.

Durnford-Slater replied that he could make very good use of it indeed. Could the brigadier send Hooper's men into South Vaagso immediately?

14

REQUESTS FOR HELP

In the grey light of early dawn everyone on *Kenya*'s bridge could see the landing craft crawling across the distant waters and approaching the shore. The bombardment was on, and the star shells briefly silhouetted the boats against the snow-covered island before it was obscured by smoke and flame. The Hampdens, abandoning their diversionary task around the Rugsundo battery, swept in to support the landings, darting towards Maaloy and South Vaagso and diving shallowly to gain speed as the pilots watched for Durnford-Slater's Verey flares to arc into the sky.

And just at that moment, with the bombardment approaching some kind of peak of fury, a loud boom and a huge water-spout near the cruiser announced the first return fire from the enemy. Was the Maaloy battery reacting so quickly?

It was not. The shot had come from Rugsundo. The Germans there, despite the harassment from the Hampdens, had spotted the "Archery" force the moment *Kenya*'s first star shell illuminated the area. A destroyer was busily making smoke between themselves and the larger vessels, but through gaps in the smokescreen they could faintly see what they later reported as "one cruiser of the Southampton class, two cruisers of the Arethusa class, and four destroyers". Landing craft were also in plain view, moving like waterbugs across the fjord towards Maaloy and South Vaagso.

The Hampdens had succeeded in knocking out one of the battery's two thirteen-centimetre Russian guns but the other was dug in too deeply to be much vulnerable. The minute the aircraft departed the German crew came out of their slit-trench, laid the gun carefully, and opened fire on the largest of the "three cruisers".

Wing-Commander Willetts, leading the Hampdens roaring in on the South Vaagso landing point, looked back and saw "what

102

looked like red-hot meteors streaking out from the . . . battery. I could watch the whole length of their flight from the mouth of the gun to the moment when they burst in the sea, when they gave off a purple smoke''.

Kenya swung one of her six-inch turrets around to engage while with the rest of her armament she continued battering Maaloy. With the help of one of the destroyers she succeeded in suppressing the German fire in about two and a half minutes. Rugsundo fell silent, but the enemy gunners on the distant island were still full of fight and would be heard from again.

In the midst of this diversion Durnford-Slater's flares appeared in the sky and a watching signalman on *Kenya*'s bridge repeated the signal to be sure the R.A.F. could not miss it. The main bombardment lifted and the Hampdens swept in and laid their smoke pots on the landing beaches. The watchers on *Kenya* had a clear view of Flight-Sergeant Smith's gallant effort to hold his machine on its final bomb run, the bomb loosed erratically creating havoc among the landing craft, and the plane finally falling off on its left wing to slide steeply down and crash into the cold waters of the fjord entrance. The troopships were the nearest vessels to the scene; signal lamps clattered on *Kenya* and *Prince Leopold*. In a moment the troopship backed out of Slaaken Bay, swung clumsily around in the narrow main channel (although fast enough, she was unusually difficult to manoeuvre for a twin-screw vessel), and churned off to the rescue.

It took perhaps ten minutes for *Prince Leopold* to reach the scene of the crash; a diesel-auxiliary fishing smack which put out from the shore as soon as the aircraft went down took slightly longer. By this time there was no sign of the wreckage but suddenly *Prince Leopold*'s bow lookout heard a weak shout from the water and spotted Smith desperately treading water in his heavy winter flying suit. They got a lifeboat away with commendable speed and pulled out Smith and two members of his crew; Smith had last seen the fourth crewman astride the wreckage in the water and supposed he had been dragged to his death when it sank. Smith was so chilled and exhausted he could hardly talk, but was otherwise unhurt. His two crewmen failed to regain consciousness, despite the best efforts of the sailors from *Prince Leopold* who took it in turn to give them artificial respiration long past the normal time limits.

The Norwegian fishing boat, *Tryoo,* swung past *Prince Leopold,* signalled a hearty welcome to the British, then turned back for shore. Later in the day two of her crew with some of their friends would row out in a small dinghy and take ship for England to join the Free Norwegian forces.

By this time things were getting pretty busy on *Kenya*'s bridge. The fighting was raging on shore and spot reports flowed into the flagship. Radio communication with Group II in South Vaagso was patchy owing to the loss of two of the Number 18 sets carried by the commandos, but an alternate system of visual signals had been arranged for just this contingency and wigwag and blinker messages from ship to shore were getting through except when drifts of smoke obscured the view.

Surprisingly little firing had been heard from the direction of Maaloy. Then suddenly fifteen more red flares arced into the sky, the prearranged signal from Major Churchill that all the guns were in British hands. The signal came as a relief to the brigadier, who had been uneasy about the ominous silence from the one quarter where the fighting ought to have been heaviest.

Four minutes later a message came in: MAALOY BATTERY AND ISLAND CAPTURED X CASUALTIES SLIGHT X DEMOLITIONS IN PROGRESS X CHURCHILL.

At about the same time one of the radiomen on the bridge overheard Clement in Halnoesvik trying to raise Durnford-Slater on the radio. There was no reply. A moment later Clement called in directly to the flagship and asked if a message could be got through to Group II: ALL GROUP 1 TASKS COMPLETED X CLEMENT. Brigadier Haydon took the message and had it passed on by semaphore code to South Vaagso. A moment later Durnford-Slater's reply came back: HEAVY RESISTANCE HERE X TELL CLEMENT BRING GROUP 1 FORWARD IMMEDIATELY X DURNFORD-SLATER.

Admiral Burrough, who had read the messages in silence as they were handed around the bridge, turned to his yeoman of signals. "Make a signal from me to *Onslow*. The Maaloy battery is in our hands. *Onslow* and *Oribi* will pass through the strait, land Group V as planned, and give fire support to the attack in the town."

Brigadier Haydon sent out another message to Jack Churchill, telling him to proceed with the demolition task at Mortenes. A moment later he ordered Henriques to send additional instructions to Maaloy: round up anyone who can be spared and get them over to the Group II landing place as quickly as possible. Churchill acknowledged and said he would send off part of 6 Troop as soon as he could get them aboard a boat.

Another message to Durnford-Slater. The floating reserve was at his disposal; did he want it sent in now and if so where? Durnford-Slater, who had just been forward for a first-hand look at the situation in the town, came up on the air—smoke was obscuring the landing beach at the moment and visual signals had been interrupted—but his message was somewhat garbled by noise. Apparently he was asking for part of the reserve troop to be sent in immediately at the Group II landing place. Radio interference was so bad that it was impossible to get an intelligible repeat on the message. The brigadier told Henriques to get one section under way immediately and keep the other standing by, and Henriques went off to talk to Hooper.

Two Me–109s appeared overhead, having taken off from Herdla at first news of the Vaagso attack. Immediately every anti-aircraft weapon in the force let fly at them and they darted off out of range; it was quite an impressive display of firepower for a pilot unaccustomed to operating around warships. But a few minutes later one of the Messerschmitts sneaked back, flying in low through the fjord entrance. (At this moment O'Flaherty and the lead section of 2 Troop were just approaching the town and it was this same aircraft that flew so close by them it nearly knocked them down.)

Suddenly the German fighter zoomed up into a steep climb, right under the tail of the Blenheim cruising overhead. The New Zealand Air Force liaison officer from Coastal Command spoke urgently into his microphone but there was no reply. Everyone on the bridge watched, helpless, as the German took position beneath the Blenheim and with one long contemptuous burst shot it out of the air. The British aircraft fell against the mountainside adjoining the fjord, exploded, and went bouncing and tumbling in a great ball of flame all the way down to the water. The deck-to-air radio link, in which Coastal Command had reposed so much confidence that they had disdained to practise it, was a complete failure insofar as the fighter umbrella was concerned. Although communication with the Hampdens (which had taken an active part in the rehearsal exercises) was excellent, the liaison officer on *Kenya* never once made contact with any of the five fighter sorties which arrived during the day. Had the crew of the hapless Blenheim been warned that the German was coming up under their machine, they might well have engaged it on less unfavourable terms.

A few minutes later Hooper started for shore with the first

section of his troop. As *Kenya*'s launches droned away towards the South Vaagso landing place, another message from Durnford-Slater arrived at the flagship: SITUATION IN NORTH END TOWN UNCERTAIN X BOTH LEAD TROOP WIRELESS SETS INOPERABLE X DURNFORD-SLATER.

Almost immediately behind this signal came another. Brigadier Haydon took the form from the signal orderly's hand and read: FAIRLY STRONG OPPOSITION ENCOUNTERED IN CENTRE AND NORTH END OF TOWN X REQUEST ALL REPEAT ALL GROUP FOUR BE SENT GROUP TWO LANDING PLACE X DURNFORD-SLATER.

Within minutes the second section of Hooper's troop was on the way to catch up with the first, whose boats were just disappearing into the smoke around the South Vaagso landing place.

15

O'FLAHERTY'S SECTION

O'Flaherty's section from 2 Troop were the first reinforcements to reach the Group II landing place. They were met on arrival by Charley Head, who was managing affairs at the C.P. while the colonel had a look at things up forward. Head told O'Flaherty to move straight up through the town, guiding generally on the main road; the colonel was up there somewhere and would have further instructions for him. O'Flaherty began moving his section up the left side of the street, passing the bodies of Sergeant Povey and Troopers Lane and Keest of 3 Troop lying where they had fallen during the early house-to-house fighting.

There was a great deal of firing going on in the town and some of it sounded very near, so O'Flaherty and his men moved with a reasonable degree of caution. Preparing to cross over to the east (fjord) side of the road, they paused a moment near the point where a drainage ditch passed underneath by means of a small culvert. O'Flaherty lined everybody up to dash across together—the approved method of crossing a fire-swept area—and as he did so heard the sound of heavy gunfire and the whistle of shells but no shellbursts. The exact source of this unusual sequence of sounds is unclear. It may have been Troopers Mapplebeck and Hannan popping away at *Föhn* with their unfused shells, or it may have been *Kenya* letting fly at the Rugsundo battery, with the sound of the shells arriving at the target masked by the high ground near Deknepol.

They sprinted across the road and took cover in the extension of the drainage ditch, a three-foot depression running from the culvert all the way down to the fjord. Ahead was an open space about the size of a pair of tennis courts, with a British body lying against the side of the building at each of the far corners; a series of small houses and sheds bordered the left side and on the right was one of the large factories extending out into the fjord.

There had still been no sign of Durnford-Slater, so O'Flaherty left most of his section in the ditch and went forward with Corporal Stenhouse and Trooper Wallineer to find out where the enemy was. Some 4 Troop men entering the factory on the right called out a warning that the open area was still under German fire. O'Flaherty and his companions dashed forward a few yards and took cover behind one of the houses on the left, which happened to be the home of the town baker.

Just across the street from the front of the house Captain Bradley was sheltering behind a similar building with some 1 Troop men, standing over the body of a trooper who had just been shot dead as he looked around the corner. Bradley shouted something at O'Flaherty and O'Flaherty shouted back but there was too much noise of gunfire and explosions for the words to carry. Exasperated, O'Flaherty made a quick dash across the street to Bradley's position and in the process just missed being shot by a wounded German lying a few yards up the street. He dived behind the corner of Bradley's house and they compared notes on the enemy situation, meanwhile exchanging occasional shots with the wounded German lying in the middle of the street. Bradley did not really know much more than O'Flaherty about the enemy situation, having just come forward himself, but he was sure of one thing: it began right where they were standing. The baker's house still seemed to be occupied by Germans; only a few minutes ago he had been fired on from the front door.

Finally someone succeeded in silencing the troublesome sniper in the street and O'Flaherty darted back to rejoin his two companions. They went around behind the baker's house and found the beginning of a narrow alley paralleling the main road behind the roadside buildings. On the opposite side of the alley was one of the outbuildings of the large fjord-side factory. Bullets cracked down the alley as they scurried around the end of the house so they took shelter in the well of a sort of semi-basement door at the bottom of a short flight of steps.

It was a very small house, really. From the open rear door in the stairwell one could see right up through the building to the front door opening on the street. A mortally wounded German lay at the head of the steps leading up to the ground floor and another enemy soldier, dead, was sprawled on the floor just inside the front entrance, shot by one of Bradley's men. There were no other Germans in the house, but the baker and his wife and a buxom daughter in a red dress were crouching uncertainly in the front room, afraid to move near the open windows; any sign of activity in the house brought a fresh fusilade from Bradley's party across the street. O'Flaherty enlisted the aid of the Norwegians and they managed to get the dying German up on a divan in one of the side rooms, making him as comfortable as possible. The man was already comatose.

Parts of the house were on fire and the baker wanted the three commandos to stay and fight the fire but O'Flaherty herded the family down into the semi-basement where they were well out of the line of fire and told them to stay there. The alley in back appeared fairly quiet now, so he posted Stenhouse and Wallineer in the stairwell to cover him and crept forward to have a look around the far corner of the factory building; he still felt that he needed more information before returning to pick up his section and bring them forward.

At the end of the alley O'Flaherty ducked quickly around the corner to the right. A German with a grenade in his hand was standing only a few yards away, looking out over the fjord. The German turned just then and the two men looked at one another with horror. Then the enemy soldier raised his arm to throw the grenade and O'Flaherty whipped up his pistol and shot him. He fell across the entrance to the factory and a second German immediately popped out the door, with another grenade. O'Flaherty fired again and missed. His gun was now empty, so he ducked back around the corner into the alley and ran for the baker's stairwell where he had left his companions. The grenade went off somewhere close behind him, hurling him violently over on his face and breaking his nose.

"I behaved like a rabbit for a few seconds," O'Flaherty remarked later. "I ran back to pick up my scarf and then rejoined Stenhouse pretty fast in the baker's back steps. Here all was not well, for Wallineer had been shot in the leg. We splinted him with his own rifle. Since we now considered the alley to be unhealthy we shoved Wallineer, the baker, his wife and daughter through the back window. The house was well and truly ablaze. The German on the couch was nearly dead and unconscious and there wasn't time to do anything for him."

O'Flaherty and Stenhouse traded shots with a sniper lying under a small building at the head of the alley and withdrew. The sniper was undoubtedly the man who had shot Wallineer, and it is puzzling that he did not also get O'Flaherty during his retreat down the alley; perhaps the grenade explosion spoiled his shot.

The enemy situation on the east side of the main road was now fairly clear. O'Flaherty's enterprising reconnaissance under fire had established that the Germans were well prepared to deal with a British advance up the fjord side of the town if the advance were made in the open. He therefore concluded that the best route of advance for his section lay through the clustered factory buildings on the waterfront.

O'Flaherty hurried back to the ditch where he had left his section and found the colonel with them. Durnford-Slater heard his report, then ordered him to move his section up the right side of the village through the factories while Bradley advanced up the left. Peter Young would arrive from Maaloy in a few minutes to take charge of the right sector and Hooper's troop was on the way in to reinforce Bradley. As the colonel turned and started off to his command post Clement appeared; he now had the rest of 2 Troop deployed among the nearby buildings. O'Flaherty repeated the report he had given the colonel and explained what Durnford-Slater wanted the troop to do; Clement told him to lead off since he already knew the ground.

As O'Flaherty was briefing his men on the situation prior to taking them forward Peter Young came up; he had just seen Durnford-Slater a moment before and knew what he was to do. O'Flaherty cautioned him about moving through the open areas and Young went back to pick up his men, whom he had left in the South Vaagso cemetery near the point where they had just landed.

O'Flaherty led his men through the outbuildings of the factory. In the first building they passed, Lieutenant Gauste of

Kompani Linge and some of Clement's men were engaged in a gunfight with a group of Germans they had cornered in an adjacent room. Without pausing, he took them all the way through the complex of buildings and reached the north end.

O'Flaherty looked out the front door of the main building. The German he had shot during his reconnaissance lay dead across the doorstep, the grenade still clutched in his hand. The bullet had caught him squarely in the chest, nearly clipping the iron cross he wore on his tunic. As O'Flaherty stood over his victim a bullet zinged in the door and nicked his shoulder, spinning him around and knocking him down. He and Trooper O'Hare, who had been standing just behind him in the doorway, scrambled clear of the opening. A moment later they were joined by Captain Young, who had picked up the men he left in the cemetery.

16

ENEMY RESISTANCE GROWS

The urgent request that he send reinforcements to South Vaagso had caught Jack Churchill at a disadvantage, for much of his force was committed to the demolition tasks on Maaloy and half of Ronald's troop had just departed for the Mortenes factory. So he called for Peter Young and told him to get as many 6 Troop soldiers as could be spared onto the boats immediately.

Young rounded up the nearest men at hand, the subsections led by Sergeants Herbert and Connolly, eighteen men in all. They hurried down to the landing-point and scrambled aboard the nearest landing craft. Some newsreel and press photographers who had accompanied Group III ashore at Maaloy ran down to the boat and asked if they might come along. Young motioned them in and the boat backed off from the beach and headed out around the southern point of the island.

As they churned across the narrow strait they could see khaki uniforms scurrying about further up the waterfront so Young told the boat officer to head north rather than directly for the Group II landing-place. They beached near a small shed across the road from the churchyard and as Young stepped ashore Charley Head appeared to greet him, shaking his hand politely like a host welcoming a guest arriving for a country weekend. Bill Etches of 1 Troop passed by, stopping to remark in a rather surprised tone that he had just been wounded in the arm.

Young heard for the first time of the deaths of Captains Giles and Forrester, and was surprised to learn of the extent of casualties in the forward troops; no news of the events in South Vaagso had been reaching Maaloy prior to his departure. While Charley Head outlined the situation, Young looked about him; it was fairly obvious that the attack had stalled, for most of the British troops in view were crouched in ditches and behind walls rather than moving ahead. Arthur Komrower hobbled by on his cane, still trying to catch up with his section. Komrower waved cheerfully and one of the men with him, catching sight of Young's detachment, called out "Good old 6 Troop!" The thought flashed through Young's mind that the situation in the town must be desperate indeed; normally, no one in 4 Troop would have a complimentary word for any other part of 3 Commando!

They went forward in search of the colonel, leaving Young's men deployed in the cemetery. Just as they departed a bullet cracked past the ear of a soldier crouching behind a gravestone. The man patted the marker and remarked wryly, "Move over, chum. I'll be with you in a minute."

Durnford-Slater was smoke-blackened and grimy, but the cheerful smile was still in place and his greeting for the newcomer was cordial. "Yeah, well, Peter, I'm glad to see you," he grinned, and the two set off to reconnoitre.

Durnford-Slater mentioned casualties, and explained the steps he had taken to get the attack moving again. Hooper's 2 Commando troop was coming ashore to help; Clement and 2 Troop, their assigned tasks around Hollevik completed, had already moved forward into South Vaagso. Hooper would move up on the left, pick up the remnants of 3 Troop, and drive north around the outskirts of the town. Bradley had brought up everyone he could spare from 1 Troop's main tasks.

"While the colonel had been speaking," Young noted later, "I had been looking around trying to make out the situation and looking for a line of advance which would offer my men at least some cover in the winter landscape. The main road was obvious-

ly covered by enemy riflemen, and the colonel said it was no
good trying to push along it. To the left the steep snow-covered
hillside at the back of the town looked forbidding. Not fifty
yards away to the right was the icy fjord.

"The colonel stopped talking and beamed at me. I expected
him to give me some particular advice, some line of advance.
There was a pause. I suggested that I should try and work
forward along the waterfront. He was obviously pleased with this
idea, which had in fact occurred to me because it seemed there
would be cover among the warehouses." It was the same thought
that had occurred to O'Flaherty.

Durnford-Slater told Young to take command of the right
sector; O'Flaherty with part of 2 Troop would come under his
orders, and was already getting into position. Having thus
outlined the task, the colonel ambled off in search of other
trouble spots.

After bumping briefly into O'Flaherty and telling the pep-
pery little lieutenant to wait for him at the north end of the
factory complex, Young returned to collect his men from the
town cemetery. They got across the open area in good order and
in a few minutes they joined O'Flaherty just inside the north
entrance of the factory, where the dead German lay across the
doorstep.

O'Flaherty told the captain what he knew of the enemy
situation and they planned their move. Ahead of them lay
another open area, perhaps seventy-five yards long. A few small
buildings and sheds bordered this area on the left and on the right
it opened directly on to the short steep slope descending to the
waters of the fjord. At the far end of the open space was a huge
red warehouse; it extended out on to a large pier jutting into the
fjord and known to the British as the "steamship wharf" from
the markings on the aerial photographs. A series of lower
structures tacked on to the left of the warehouse and contiguous
with it extended its length all the way to the main road so that it
lay, an unavoidable obstacle, across the path of the British
advance. Snipers were firing from somewhere within the buildings.

Nearer at hand, not more than twenty yards from the
doorway where the two officers were crouched, a small building
stood on pilings which raised its floor a few feet above the
ground. It was from beneath this building, apparently some sort
of storage shed, that the concealed sniper covered the alleyway
behind the baker's house. Off farther to the left and beyond,

closer to the warehouse itself, something moved in the window of a yellow house.

Young decided to advance by bounds up the left side of the exposed area, with the raised shed as his first objective. Before moving, he took two men with a Bren gun and positioned them in the window directly above the factory doorway, where they could give covering fire during the attack. Then he led off in a wild rush for the cover of the first shed.

They gained the south wall of the shed without incident but there was no opening to give access to the interior. Young edged around to the street side of the building—and saw two Germans duck into the doorway. He shouted "Hande hoch!" but nothing happened.

A dark-haired and athletic trooper named Sherington crowded past Young with a tommy gun and crouched in front of the doorway. Firing from the hip, he emptied his magazine into the opening and sprang back to reload. But the Germans within had been suitably impressed; as Sherington got ready to administer another dose they poked out a piece of white cloth and then came filing out with their hands over their heads: two soldiers and a sailor, followed by the frightened Norwegian who owned the shed. One of the soldiers turned out to be Alexander Holscher, a popular singer in prewar operatic spectacles.

The north end of the shed was enclosed by an L-shaped lumber pile, about chin-high to an average man, which formed a kind of enclosed yard. Young and his men herded their prisoners into this space and crowded in after them, getting into position for the final dash to the near wall of the red warehouse. O'Flaherty and his own detachment had by this time bolted across the open space behind Young and they too crowded into the tiny woodyard. Every now and then the Germans in the red warehouse spattered the woodpile with bullets.

It was getting very congested in the narrow enclosure; Durnford-Slater, who came galloping forward to join Young and O'Flaherty just then, estimated there must have been thirty men jammed into the tiny enclosure. The noise level was approaching some kind of a peak: rifles and machine-guns were rattling; tommy guns popped and stuttered in the town and were answered by the rapid drilling sound of German Schmeissers; out in the fjord the Rugsundo battery had just exploded a round against *Kenya*'s armour plating and the cruiser was angrily replying with all her main batteries; a flight of German aircraft appeared

"Schmeisser" (MP-40)

overhead and all the ships cut loose at them until three Beaufighters snarled in to engage; a series of huge explosions shook the whole town as Lieutenant Etches' 1 Troop demolitionists knocked down one of the factories. Durnford-Slater, leaving the headquarters signallers crouched over their radio sets trying fruitlessly to make out an incoming message, heard one of them cry out, "This is bloody awful! A man can't even hear himself think!"

And then there was absolute silence, one of those sudden calms which occur unexpectedly during a battle when the birds can be heard twittering in the trees. Out in the fjord an officer on one wing of *Kenya*'s bridge was bellowing at a damage control party just below, trying to make himself heard over the terrible cacophony of combat. The awful racket died away without warning and he was left screaming into a dead calm. To the delight of the brigadier and his staff, Admiral Burrough gave the man a look of mild annoyance and, turning to Captain Denny, said in a shocked tone, "Flags, tell that young officer to *moderate* his voice."

In the woodyard, the sudden silence was as suddenly broken. Two shots cracked out. A sergeant standing next to Durnford-Slater slumped to the ground, blood bubbling at his lips. Trooper Clark spun around, clutching at his left arm, and cried out that he had been shot from behind. Everyone felt jumpy and Durnford-Slater says he himself was genuinely frightened for the first time that day, though no change of expression betrayed his feeling. Then someone spotted a German helmet in the window of a bypassed house and a storm of fire tore the window-frame to shreds; the helmet jerked and fell back out of sight.

Captain Young sent the wounded Clark with another trooper to herd the prisoners to the rear. They scurried across the open space with their charges and vanished into the factory building. Nothing could be done for the wounded sergeant, a 2 Troop man named Hughes; the shot had passed through both lungs and he lay on his back, dying. More German bullets from the red warehouse ahead snapped and cracked into the woodyard. Plainly it would be fatal to tarry there.

"We must get on," prompted the colonel.

Young and O'Flaherty squinted carefully over the woodpile, scanning the German position. There seemed no available route offering any sort of cover. Young sensed that every moment's delay gave the Germans more time to get ready; if anything were to be done it had better be done quickly.

The red warehouse was nearly fifty yards away. Regretfully, Young looked back at the north wall of the shed behind him: not so much as a loophole from which his troop sniper might give covering fire. He stood up.

"We'll get in there and reorganize," he shouted, pointing at the red warehouse. "Come on!" Like an olympic sprinter leaving the blocks he bolted out into the open, but it was hard running in the snow. Later he recounted his sensations of the moment:

"It was pretty plain that the only chance of getting away with this move was to make it fast. Despite the snow and my haversack full of bombs I was making pretty good time. Suddenly a smart-looking German in a long overcoat, steel helmet and equipment stepped into the doorway—now little more than ten yards away—and flung a stick grenade at me. It fell some ten feet to my right. I fired from the hip as I ran, swerving to the left; a second grenade followed the first, bursting in almost the same place. By this time I had reached the wall of the building and there was only a large wooden crate between me and the doorway. Within seconds George Herbert and Sergeant Connolly had joined me, and the rest were coming up at the double. Whilst we were still fumbling for our Mills grenades a stick bomb flew out of the door and fell about eight feet away. My legs will be full of bits, I thought. It did not go off. Perhaps the German forgot to pull the pin.''

The last panting stragglers in this wild dash slammed into the wall and flattened themselves against the building. With a massed cry of *"Hande hoch!"* (the only German most of them knew), the whole group began heaving grenades in the door. There was no reply. Confident that no German inside could have survived a full dozen bursting grenades, Captain Young walked in. He found himself in a narrow hallway running along the front wall; on the right a flight of stairs led up to the second storey, and straight ahead another door opened into a darkened inner room. The walls were pockmarked with grenade splinters but there was no sign of the Germans. Silhouetted in the doorway, Young peered uncertainly into the second room. From the far corner two shots flashed out and he sprang back out the main door into the snow, a bullet appearing magically on the door behind him.

A frontal assault on the main entrance appeared out of the question, so the British soldiers spread out along the front of the buildings looking for alternate means of entry. Up towards the street there was a sudden rustle of movement in the extension to the main building. Someone flung a grenade in the window. The explosion was followed by a flurry of stamping and banging mixed with the whinnying of terrified horses. The outbuilding was a stable.

There was no second entrance to the main warehouse from the south side. Disgustedly, Young stared at the high wooden walls, wondering how in the world the obstacle could be breached. And then the light dawned.

Wooden! Burn it down! He sent Sergeant Herbert after a bucket of petrol.

But as Young was getting his fire-assault organized and a detail of his men led the frightened horses out of the stable,

Tommy Gun

O'Flaherty's patience with the Germans ran out. He had already suffered two light wounds, and he was fighting mad. Borrowing a tommy gun from a nearby soldier, he checked that it was fully loaded and then darted forward through the front door. Trooper Sherington impulsively followed him and Captain Young, feeling that as senior officer present he ought to take part in whatever action developed, went in at their heels.

Inside it was still dark, a disconcerting contrast to eyes grown accustomed to the glare of sun on the snow outside. As Young burst through the door two shots rang out and O'Flaherty and Sherington toppled to the floor. Young fired at the flash of the German guns and for the second time ducked back out of the building.

Firing the building simply would not do now, for O'Flaherty

and Sherington might still be alive inside. As if to confirm this, Sherington's voice gasped out that he had been shot from the second room.

Young held a council of war outside the building, soliciting ideas from his sergeants. The only suggestion that showed any promise was to seek out some way of getting directly into the upstairs and then shooting down through the floor at the Germans while they were pinned down by covering fire through the main entrance. But this depended on finding a way in, and there seemed to be none.

Within the building O'Flaherty too was still alive, although horribly wounded; a German bullet had broken his jaw, split his palate, and taken out one eye. As he had entered the building he caught a quick glimpse, barely an impression, of the flight of stairs to his right and the door opening into the dark room beyond.

"I heard a shot," says O'Flaherty, "and as my companion fell I was thrown to my knees against the outside wall by a blow on my head. When I had stopped seeing stars and got up and picked up my gun I saw a figure in the door and he fired—how long then elapsed I have no idea. I came to on my face. My brain was quite clear. The flashing lights had passed and I remember looking at my hands which were moving themselves with pins and needles. I sat up against the wall and saw the two Germans near me, ignoring me but peering through a window. My tommy gun had gone. I heaved myself up and together with Sherington walked out. I believe our two companions were glad to see the end of us."

They should not have been, because departure of the two wounded Britishers opened the door once more to Peter Young's plan to set fire to the building.

The soldiers pressed against the outside wall were surprised to see O'Flaherty and Sherington stagger out the door. The thought flashed through Young's mind that O'Flaherty looked as if he had had a plate of strawberry jam thrown in his face. Trooper Hannan caught the lieutenant as he collapsed and someone else grabbed Sherington. O'Flaherty's brain was still clear but he was in shock. When he tried to explain the situation of the Germans inside the building he could only stammer, and Young peered at him closely and said, "Someone take this man to the rear."

The plan to set fire to the warehouse was put into effect.

The remaining horses were led from the stables and Lance-Sergeant Herbert heaved a bucketful of petrol in through the main entrance. A grenade followed and the building burst into flames. Young left Lance-Corporal Fyson with a Bren gun to cover the blazing warehouse and swung off with the rest of his detachment. A short time later the two Germans made a run for it and Fyson dropped them in their tracks.

Meanwhile, Captain Hooper's reserve troop had come forward and joined the action. Hooper sent one section under Lieutenant Jack Vanderwerve to reinforce Young in the righthand sector, while the other section under Lieutenant G. D. Black made a wide swing through the left side of the town, picking up the remnants of 3 Troop and some of Bradley's men as they swept by. Hooper and the troop headquarters section guided straight up the road, moving carefully through the centre of the town.

German snipers armed with automatic rifles were still very much in action and the troop quickly came under heavy fire. Lieutenant Black took a wing shot at two fleeing Germans whereupon one of them, armed with a Schmeisser machine pistol, swung around and ripped off a quick burst, wounding Black in the forearm.[1]

The ubiquitous Durnford-Slater moved back and forth through the areas where the hottest fighting was taking place. He seemed to bear a charmed life as he walked up the main road, armed only with a .45 pistol. Bullets cracked and zipped amongst the buildings of the town. A few messengers stayed with Durnford-Slater wherever he went, and to his side and one pace behind stalked Sergeant Mills, an ex-Army Championship boxer who had appointed himself the colonel's bodyguard for the day.

Suddenly the door of a house opened as the colonel walked by and a grenade rolled out right at his feet. There was an explosion and he flew through the air and vanished; his two orderlies were seriously wounded. Peter Young, watching from across the street, knew that his commander had been killed.

But a moment later Durnford-Slater reappeared, apparently unhurt. He had seen the grenade just in time and concurrently

---

[1] A few months later Black happened to be teaching enemy weapons to a class of commando recruits in Scotland. When one of his charges inquired about the accuracy of the Schmeisser, Black turned back his sleeve and drawled, "Well, I reckon a two-inch group at a hundred yards isn't too bad."

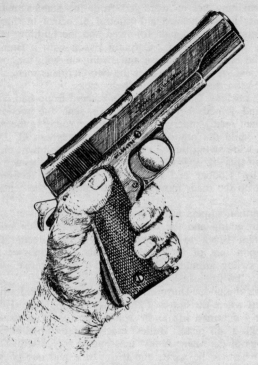

.45 Pistol

with the explosion had made a fastastic dive into the cover of the
next doorway, suffering nothing worse than skinned knuckles in
the process. As he rose to his feet the door from whence the
grenade had issued opened once more and a German sailor
emerged, his hands over his head. The enraged Mills raised his
weapon. The German shrank back in terror and cried, *"Nein,
nein!"*

"Ja, ja," said Mills, and shot him.

It was not a time for considering the finer points of ethics,
and the German had after all prefaced his surrender with an
attempt on the colonel's life. Durnford-Slater simply shrugged

his shoulders and said, "Yeah, well, Mills, you shouldn't have
done that." Then he walked off.

17

DEMOLITIONS

As Number 3 Commando's administrative officer, "Slinger"
Martin was ostensibly a non-combatant, but his restless nature
rebelled at the prospect of confining itself to routine tasks while
the unit was engaged in action. It did not take him long to
discover suitable outlets for his excess energy.

Martin's first duty upon landing was to get the reserve
ammunition unloaded from the boats and set up a dump atop the
cliff above the Group II landing-place. This he did, working
alongside his quartermaster-sergeant and two storesmen, while
hoarse shouts, explosions and the rattle of tommy guns just
around the bend in the road signalled that 3 and 4 Troops had
come up against the first German positions south of the town.
Martin and his crew continued with their work, sorting out the
ammunition and breaking it down into man-transportable loads to
be carried to the forward troops; they hoped eventually to find
some obliging Norwegians to serve as carrying parties.

Gradually the sounds of the fighting moved farther away,
although the occasional stray bullet sang by as the Germans fired
blindly into the smoke obscuring the landing-point. The battle of
Maaloy had already ended, and there was a tremendous blast as
one of Lieutenant Brandwood's demolition parties dealt with the
German battery's ammunition stores. As Martin and his men
were finishing their first task, Captain Bill Bradley of 1 Troop
came back to the landing-point and asked if Martin and his men
could take over one of the troop's demolition tasks. German
resistance south of the town was unexpectedly stiff and Bradley
wanted to divert more of his Group II demolition parties to
assist 3 and 4 Troops in the main assault.

Martin and Bradley went off with Sergeant Miller, the "Q"
sergeant, to have a look at the target, the large canning factory

adjacent to the landing-place. It was a big modern building of iron and concrete, owned by one of the more notorious local quislings, and if there were any doubt that the British landing had taken the town by surprise the doubt was removed when they entered the factory offices. The staff had obviously cleared out in alarm; papers were still lying on the desks, and filing cabinets stood open along the wall.

Bradley went off about his business, and Martin and Miller began planning the destruction of the factory. They collected all the papers and files they could find, stuffing them by the armload into sacks and setting them outside the building to be carried back to London for examination by the intelligence specialists. It seemed a waste to let perfectly good typewriters go up with the building since they were at that time in short supply back in England (Napoleon's dictum notwithstanding, a modern army marches as much upon its paper as its stomach), so several prime specimens were "liberated" for the use of His Britannic Majesty's forces. Then Miller and Martin proceeded to the basement and took measurements of certain structural members for reference in calculating the size of their charges. Heavy fighting was still going on nearby, and the rattle and bang of combat was punctuated by occasional crashes as stray bullets shattered windows in the factory.

The basic calculations done, they returned to the landing place to collect the requisite amounts of explosives. Trooper Mainwaring helped them lug a considerable weight of demolitions back to the building and lay the charges for firing when the landing force withdrew.

Durnford-Slater, who seemed to be everywhere that day, wandered into the building to see how the project was going. A Norwegian civilian also got in somehow and began busying himself around some of the machinery, a little too intent on his meaningless tasks. The colonel looked at him suspiciously, then sent for an interpreter.

"Go find out what that man thinks he's doing in here," he said. "He'll have to get out. We're preparing to destroy the building."

"Why, I know that man," said the colonel's interpreter, a native of the area. "That's the local chairman of the *Nasjonal Samling* party, Johann Gotteborg. He owns this place."

The luckless collaborator was promptly taken into custody and marched to the landing place to await a trip to England. He was one of the two men the landing force had specific instructions to arrest.

The colonel remarked to Martin that ammunition, in particular hand grenades, was already running short among the troops fighting in the streets of the town. By this time a number of young Norwegians had collected around the landing-place, hoping to get passage back to England where they might join the Free Norwegian armed forces, so Martin asked for volunteers for carrying parties. Most of the Norwegians agreed enthusiastically; they were eager to help the British in any way they could. Martin broke the volunteers down into three gangs and loaded each man with sacks and boxes of ammunition. Leaving Trooper Blackwood to guard the supply dump, Martin, Miller and Mainwaring each took one of the groups and went forward to resupply the front-line elements. They panted up the main road, stumbling and sliding in the snow with their heavy loads, and soon reached the lower portion of the town. Martin's party ran into Peter Young and his detachment coming over from Maaloy and replenished their ammunition supply while Young went forward in search of the colonel. Then they went on to Bradley's position. A few yards away Mainwaring was setting up a forward dump for what was left of 3 Troop. Suddenly rifle fire began to smack into the ground all around the carrying parties; everyone dived for cover.

At this moment the ubiquitous Durnford-Slater came scurrying up again, his orderlies trotting at his heels. He slid into a covered position beside Martin and took stock of the situation.

Trooper Allen, the colonel's runner, spotted the source of the enemy fire. There were some Germans up among a cluster of tiny huts on the hillside to the west of the town.

"This won't do," said the colonel. "Martin, get those bastards out of there, and blow up the huts." And having thus spoken, he scrambled out into the open again and he and Allen went off about their own pursuits.

1 and 3 Troops had finished distributing the fresh ammunition amongst themselves and disappeared among the buildings of the town, so the impatient Martin had to send Mainwaring back to the landing-place for more grenades. Meanwhile the greyhaired "non-combatant" conferred briefly with a 1 Troop Brengunner who happened to have taken up a position nearby, and explained what he planned to do. Mainwaring came back with not only grenades, but a reinforcement: Blackwood, the second

Bren Gun

storesman, had refused to sit idly at the landing-place while his friends got into action. The German snipers were still firing.

At Martin's signal the Bren-gunner emptied a full magazine into the huts. Under cover of this diversion, the four-man "Q" section dashed forward and scrambled up the rocky slope to the first of the buildings. They paused for a moment to catch their breath, then scuttled quickly across the remaining open space to the two huts from which the German fire had issued. As they flattened themselves against the outer wall of the first hut someone moved noisily inside the structure.

Mainwaring crawled carefully around the base of the hut towards the entrance. Suddenly he jerked up his tommy gun and fired a quick burst.

"There's two of them in there," he called over his shoulder. Martin let fly with a Mills bomb from a range of about ten yards, and followed it up immediately with an incendiary grenade. The first missile sailed neatly in the window and exploded, but the concussion threw the captain's aim off and the incendiary bounced harmlessly off the wall and fell to the ground. But it still burst close enough to set the wooden portion of the hut (pitch-soaked pinewood) alight.

As the building blazed up the commandos ducked across into the cover of the third hut, speeded on their way by a tattoo of Bren fire rattling past their ears; this last structure turned out to be empty. The two Germans in the second hut made a break for it when the flames grew too hot and were cut down by the alert Bren-gunner.

Meanwhile, Lieutenant Clement and the remainder of his troop, arriving belatedly from Hollevik, had gone into action and were well and truly engaged. While O'Flaherty's section went off with Young's 6 Troop on the right (fjord) side of the main road, Clement had sent Chatton's section on a wide swing through the left side of the village, warning them not to get *too* far left since troops in British uniforms, presumably Hooper's men, could be seen working along the hillside around the flank of the German defence. This left Clement with only six men, mostly troop headquarters types, but he resolved to get the attack going again in 4 Troop's sector, picking up the scattered parties from that troop as he went forward.

4 Troop's attack had come to a complete halt, and small parties of men lay pinned down by German fire here and there, occasionally rising up to get off a few shots, then being driven back into cover. Clement started gathering these men into his little task force. They worked their way around behind the cluster of buildings comprising the two small hotels and attendant annexes, garages and sheds. Almost immediately they ran into a group of Germans ensconced in one of the buildings. This particular group was not doing much firing (the Germans too were running low on ammunition in the centre of the town), but every attempt by a British soldier to approach the building called forth a rain of grenades which quickly drove him back into cover.

If any assault on the building were to have a chance of success, fire support of some kind would be needed. Clement took inventory and found that his little group disposed of rifles, pistols, grenades and a single tommy gun. Aside from these weapons they had nothing but a two-inch mortar whose ammunition supply, excepting a few smoke bombs, had been exhausted, and a Verey pistol for signalling. The first approach to the problem at hand was obviously the smoke rounds, so the mortar was set up forthwith and registered on the target. But smoke does not kill, and even though a few rounds crashed accurately through the roof of the building the Germans showed no sign of weakening; they still did their very best to exterminate anyone who approached their position. The next scheme involved setting fire to the building by firing Verey flares in the windows. This too was a failure; even when a few flares actually got into the building—no mean trick, as the Verey pistol is a signalling device only and is not meant to be fired for accuracy—they did not start a fire and did nothing to dampen the Germans' enthusiasm.

The only remaining alternative was a sudden charge on the building, in hopes of getting close enough for some offensive grenade work. Clement and Lance-Sergeant Culling lined up the men and at Clement's signal they all broke from cover and ran at the Germans, Culling and Clement in the lead. They got as far as a little swale about fifteen yards from the door of the structure before a man stepped into the opening and threw a single grenade which hit Culling squarely in the face and exploded, killing him instantly. As Clement ducked, a shower of grenades came from the doorway and adjacent windows and the other men were driven back, leaving the lieutenant alone near the building, pinned down by a German who sniped him every time he raised his head.

The others made a second attempt on the building, and again were driven off. They shouted to Clement that they could not get to him and he chose to temper valour with discretion. Under cover of a spattering of small-arms fire from his companions, he jumped to his feet and retired unscathed, after which he sent off a runner to ask for fire support of some kind.

In a few minutes the runner returned with Sergeant Ramsay and the three-inch mortar crew from Bradley's 1 Troop.

The building which Clement had been unable to reach contained the German harbourmaster's office, and was serving as a collecting station for German casualties. Leutnant zur See Sebelin was inside, and might well have been driven out by this time but for the wounded men; he wanted to get them out safely before withdrawing, at which time he would have to set fire to the office files, and the whole building would probably go up in flame. But Ramsay's first shell crashed through the roof before the evacuation was complete, killing some of the wounded men lying on the floor. As the mortar shells continued to rain in the surviving Germans lit their fire and went out the back way.

A huge explosion somewhere off to the right threw flaming chunks of wood and miscellaneous debris high into the air, starting a whole series of fires in the centre of the town. Lieutenant Etches, who had just done a demolitions course a few weeks earlier and believed in using explosives liberally to make sure of destroying the target, was dealing with the Steamship Wharf. Vast billows of smoke rolled through the streets and alleyways, and the combined heat of dozens of blazing structures drove back British and Germans alike. Clement had by this time

collected a sizeable assault party but now the intense heat
frustrated all efforts to get the attack moving again. He got his
men spread out and settled down to wait for the fires to burn
lower.

Interlude

HERDLA

It had been a busy morning at Herdla aerodrome.

There were only nine planes on the field and each morning,
before anyone could fly, engines had to be warmed up and petrol
tanks topped off again. Here as in England there was a coating of
snow and ice on the wings and control surfaces today. Two of the
station's Me–109Fs were kept always at the ready for take-off,
but there was little sense of urgency about pre-flighting the other
serviceable machines; few enemy aircraft ever ventured so far
from home base as Norway.

The first alert sounded shortly after dawn, when the duty
officer at 69th Division headquarters rang through to report
enemy activity around Vaagso Island, eighty miles up the coast
in the sector of the neighbouring 181st Division. British aircraft
were attacking the coast defence batteries at Halsoer, Maaloy and
Rugsundo, and some kind of landing was taking place.

The two Me–109s standing by on ground alert took off
immediately, while ground crews hurriedly began preflight preparation of the remaining fighters. It was more than thirty minutes
to the operational area, and before the first two pilots had even
reached the target another alert call came in from Bergen. British
aircraft were attacking a coastal convoy five miles south-west of
Eigeroy, and all the fighters at Stavanger had been "scrambled";
could the commandant at Herdla send any machines?

This second action was within the 69th Division's zone of
responsibility, whereas the Vaagso area was not. So the balance
of the Messerschmitts from Herdla roared off to the south rather
than the north. After defending the convoy, they would have to
refuel at Stavanger before returning to their home base.

Ju 88

Later in the morning word was received that the attack on the convoy had been beaten off, and twin-engined fighters from Stavanger would begin shuttling north to attack the enemy formations at Vaagso, using Herdla as a refuelling stop. A flight of two Ju-88s swooped down, topped off their tanks, and roared off again to the north.

The first two Me–109s returned from the northern battle area, bumping down on the plank runway and taxied in to refuel. The pilots were excited; there were British warships all over the fjord, they reported, with enemy aircraft circling above them. They had seen at least four Blenheims, of which number they had destroyed one and crippled another which was last seen running for home with an Me–110 from Trondheim in pursuit. The anti-aircraft fire from the ships had been very intense, but the pilots asked that their aircraft be refuelled and rearmed immediately so that they might take off on another sortie.

The ground staff finished their work, and the first Me–109 taxied quickly out to the end of the runway, while the second pilot strapped himself into his cockpit. The operations N.C.O. cleared the first aircraft for take-off. As it zoomed off the end of the wooden runway and the second machine taxied out to follow he automatically noted the time in the station logbook: 1159 exactly. At that very moment a flak gun barked nearby, and suddenly every anti-aircraft battery in the area opened up. Low on the horizon, swooping in from the sea, came thirteen Blenheim bombers, lined up perfectly on the single runway as though preparing to land. They roared in across the field at 250-foot altitude, bomb bays open; 250-lb bombs and small incendiaries showered down on the huts and runway. One pass and they were gone, while planks, mud, and splinters of wood and steel flew into the air. Gaping holes opened in the wooden runway, one of them directly in front of the taxiing fighter which skidded forward into the smoking crater and upended. Dispersal huts and sections of the runway surface burst into flame.

As the enemy bombers roared off the target one of them took a direct hit from an 88mm shell and lurched violently to one side, colliding with its neighbour. The two crippled machines spiralled awkwardly down and crashed into the sea. Their mates disappeared over the horizon towards Scotland.

More than twenty huge craters gaped in the single wooden runway. The station at Herdla was closed, and would be for several days while repair crews made good the damage. A convenient refuelling stop no longer existed between Stavanger and Vaagso. Herdla and Stavanger were effectively out of the game: for the rest of the day, the "Archery" force would have to reckon only with those Luftwaffe aircraft capable of making the long round trip from Trondheim.

Herdla's busiest day had ended at one minute after noon, exactly.

18

DESTROYERS IN ACTION

Having received the admiral's order to run through the Maaloy Strait and penetrate the upper fjord, Captain Armstrong got *Onslow* and *Oribi* under way immediately. At 0941, *Oribi* in the lead with Birney's commandos standing by to man their boat stations and *Onslow* close behind with Armstrong peering into the dense smoke ahead from his position on her bridge, they swept grandly into the narrow passage between the smaller and the larger island. A few yards to their right a German hut blazed fiercely; those above deck could feel the heat, so closely did they pass. A literal stone's throw to their left was South Vaagso, where khaki-clad figures could be seen dodging and shooting amongst the wooden buildings. Boiling ahead over the mirror-like waters, they passed the leading commando elements and the flank of the improvised German defensive line. The startled Germans swung around and plastered them with small-arms fire as they passed, and *Oribi*'s crew took three minor casualties.

And then suddenly they emerged from the smoke overhanging the strait, and the whole panorama of Ulvesund lay before them. Two good-sized merchant ships under full steam were dashing up-channel towards the northern exit, with an armed trawler snapping along at their heels like a sheep dog bringing the flock in to dinner. Armstrong ordered his signalmen to challenge, and the trawler opened fire.

The armed trawler was the German patrol boat *Föhn*, and her skipper, Leutnant zur See Lohr, had already had enough thrills that morning to last the average seaman a year. *Föhn*, one of the little 250-ton fishing vessels modified by the Germans to serve as coast patrol boats and armed escorts for small convoys, had been told off for the latter duty on this particular day. The three steamers she was to accompany (S.S. *Eismeer*, 1,000 tons; S.S. *Norma*, 2,200 tons; S.S. *Reimer Etzard Fritzen*, 3,000 tons) were just getting up steam in the harbour north of Maaloy when the first British aircraft appeared overhead and every anti-aircraft gun in the vicinity opened up. Lohr's gunners joined in the barrage, and it was probably the tracer curling upward from their guns that Clement had seen from his boat station on *Prince Leopold*, appearing from his point of view to be rising out of the intervening hilltop. The trawler did not carry any really heavy armament, but her twin Oerlikons could put out an impressive volume of fire.

Nine minutes later, when *Kenya*'s star shell lit the sky and the ferocious bombardment of Maaloy began, *Föhn*'s crewmen were nearly blown overboard by the concussion; the trawler was anchored very close to the north shore of the island. But when the bombardment lifted and the second flight of Hampdens swept in at low altitude to smoke the landing places it was one of *Föhn*'s guns that put the fatal round into Flight-Sergeant Smith's port engine; the gunners cheered when Smith's Hampden suddenly streamed smoke, fell off on its left wing as the bomb dropped clear, and disappeared behind the hills south of the town.

But a few minutes later Lohr realized that his ship was in *real* trouble. Small-arms fire and grenade explosions resounded from the nearby island, and it quickly became apparent that they were coming closer. Obviously an enemy landing of some sort had taken place, and *Föhn* was sitting right next to one of the prime objectives. As Peter Young's men broke over the hilltop and dashed downslope towards the smoking buildings on the near shore Lohr concluded that he had better get his convoy moving fast. Signalling to the steamers to slip anchor and run north at flank speed, he directed his quartermaster to position *Föhn* between the island and the fleeing ships, and ordered his gunners to open fire on the British troops. *Norma* and *Fritzen* obeyed promptly enough, but the flat-bottomed schuyt *Eismeer*, moored 2,000 metres north of the island near the Trolleboflu lighthouse, still had not raised enough pressure in her boilers to turn over the engines. She bobbed helplessly at anchor.

Fohn's gunners sprayed the approaching commandos with machine-gun fire. Then, as *Norma* and *Fritzen* gathered speed up-fjord, Lohr put his helm hard over and swung away from the island to follow, just as Troopers Mapplebeck and Hannan swung their captured gun around on its traverse mounting and brought it to bear. A moment later there was a boom from the island and a small splash near *Föhn*, then several more. Finally one of the explosions was echoed by a splintering crash somewhere below deck as an unfused shell punched through *Föhn*'s side. A second round banged through the hull without exploding and then surprisingly (but to the immense relief of the shaken German seamen) the British fire ceased.

But *Föhn*'s ordeal had only begun. Now as she swung her bows to the north and boiled away after her two consorts she succeeded in opening the range by only a few thousand yards before a British destroyer nosed out of the smoke obscuring the Maaloy Strait, her signal lamp blinking out a challenge. Another destroyer emerged, only seconds behind the first.

Thinking fast, *Eismeer*'s crew broke out a Dutch flag. For the moment, the ruse worked; the British destroyers surged out of the gap like hounds catching sight of a fox, intent on the prizes disappearing around Brandhaevnes Point to the north. They payed no attention to the helpless *Eismeer*. Norwegians watching from both sides of the fjord waved and cheered as the British vessels, battle ensigns fluttering proudly, cracked a shot across the bows of the two merchantmen and took *Föhn* under fire.

The game was up, but Lohr was a man of resolution and would play it out to the end. Ordering his gunners to open fire on the pursuing destroyers, he signalled to the steamers to beach themselves immediately to avoid being sunk. *Norma* turned hard to port, heeling over violently, and rammed into the shore at full speed; *Fritzen,* just beyond her, did the same. *Föhn,* pounded by the British guns but still spitting bullets defiantly, ploughed past them and then turned hard for the shore.

Lohr ran back into the tiny radio room behind his bridge and scooped up the confidential code books; in accordance with world-wide naval practice, the books were bound in lead so they could be dropped overboard in the event capture seemed imminent. With the codes under his arm, Lohr dashed back out on to the bridge, and straight into a storm of British fire. A bursting shell from one of *Onslow*'s guns caught him and he crumpled across the rail, the books dropping from his hands; he was dead before they hit the deck. *Föhn* crunched into the shore, and her surviving crew members grabbed rifles and leapt ashore.

Oribi went right on by, continuing up the sound to land Birney's detachment near North Vaagso as planned. But *Onslow* hove to near the beached vessels, and lowered her whaler with a boarding party under Lieutenant-Commander A. N. P. de Costabadie, D.S.C., R.N., a cool veteran who had brought one of the last motor launches away from Dunkirk and now served on Mountbatten's Combined Operations Planning Staff, where he had been one of the principal architects of the present operation.

De Costabadie ordered the whaler alongside *Föhn* first, and he and two seamen climbed over the rail but immediately had to duck for cover as bullets spattered around them and whanged off the trawler's fittings. *Föhn* means phoenix in German, and this one was already rising from its ashes; the survivors of Lohr's crew shared their late captain's fighting spirit, and they were damned well ready to fight from the shore if they were unable to go on fighting from their ship. Having jumped ashore with rifles and pistols and concealed themselves among some scattered rocks, they now set about sniping methodically at the British boarding party.

De Costabadie seized a rifle lying on the deck, presumably dropped there by one of the crew in his haste to get ashore, and fired at the Germans from behind the trawler's wooden lifeboat, but they kept on shooting back. *Onslow*'s gunnery officer, an aggressive young lieutenant named Macro Wilson, decided to pitch in and help, so he carefully trained the destroyer's forward guns on the German positions and said "Fire". The result was something more than the Germans in their hasty positions could endure, so after a few minutes of this treatment they gave up and withdrew down the coastal road towards South Vaagso, where they could presumably find someone to fight on more even terms. The boarding party made a quick search of the trawler, noting with respect that Lohr had died in the very act of getting rid of his code books.

Lohr's code books were the major intelligence find of the Vaagso raid, and were to prove invaluable to the Royal Navy during future operations. They identified by radio call sign every German vessel in Norway and France and listed a whole series of challenges, countersigns and emergency signals. It was with the help of these codes that another commando force got into the heavily defended St. Nazaire docks a few months later.

De Costabadie picked up the books and he and his party climbed back into the whaler and moved off to the next beached vessel, *Fritzen*. As they rowed across the intervening space a second boarding party from *Onslow* under Sub-Lieutenant M. P. Vaux went ashore and in less than five minutes captured seventeen German seamen who had escaped from the beached vessels.

Nothing of any great value was found on board *Fritzen*. De Costabadie went to the captain's cabin, where he underwent something of a traumatic experience. His curiosity aroused by a securely padlocked cupboard, he blew the lock away with his revolver—only to find that his bullets had smashed all three bottles of the expensive brandy hidden inside.

The boarding party moved on again. By now it was well past noon, but the supposed Dutch vessel, the schuyt *Eismeer*, still rode peacefully at anchor. Her crew had long since abandoned ship and scattered ashore, but the vessel's proximity to the northern edge of the town brought it under the effective protection of the German garrison. As the whaler's crew pulled for *Eismeer*, a German bullet hit the seaman manning the stroke oar and he fell mortally wounded into the bottom of the boat. De Costabadie and his party got aboard the schuyt successfully, and it seemed a perfect opportunity to take the undamaged vessel as a prize, a contingency foreseen and encouraged by the naval operation order for the raid. *Eismeer* stood free for the taking, and all that remained was to hoist anchor and sail or tow her away.

But there was one very small snag, and it proved once again the validity of the cockney sailor's lament that "it's the little things wot mucks yer up". The capstan used for raising the anchor was situated in a particularly exposed position on the foredeck, and every time someone ventured out to crank it he met with such a hail of rifle fire from the shore that he had to scamper back quickly into the shelter of the deckhouse. Lieutenant Wilson on *Onslow*, hopeful of repeating his earlier success against the beached firebrands of *Föhn*'s crew, trained all his armament on the hillside behind the vessel, whence the sniper fire seemed to be issuing, and on the German positions in the northern portion of the town, which Durnford-Slater's men still had not succeeded in reaching. *Onslow* laid down a heavy curtain of fire in an effort to smother the snipers, but to no avail. These Germans were made of sterner stuff; they leaned into the naval gunfire and stubbornly kept on taking potshots at anyone who dared expose himself on *Eismeer*'s deck. The combined fury of pompoms, machine guns, Oerlikons, Lewis guns and even the main armament could not dislodge them, and they continued to beat back every British attempt on the crucial capstan. Captain Armstrong finally realized that he was stalemated, and called back his boarding party. About the only thing he had not done to the Germans was take his ship ashore and ram them, and now they began adding insult to injury by sniping at his own crewmen on the decks of the destroyer itself. Startled sailors found themselves involved in an infantry engagement without leaving their battle positions on the ship.

Onslow's main guns kept banging away at the Germans until the boarding party was safely re-embarked, and then the disgusted Armstrong gave orders to sink *Eismeer* where she lay. Wilson's gunners ripped a great chunk out of her lower hull and the schuyt settled to the bottom. *Onslow* lay just off shore and continued firing at the Germans on the island, the while punching holes in the beached vessels to ensure that they would not be easily refloated.

During the *Eismeer* fracas a singular event had taken place which would prove a source of great pride to *Onslow*'s crew for years to come. An ancient four-inch gun had recently been fitted on the ship's afterdeck in place of a bank of torpedo tubes, in hope of increasing her anti-aircraft protection by however small a margin. While all the main armament was banging away at the German snipers harassing de Costabadie's party, a German aircraft appeared overhead. Wilson trained this venerable museum piece skyward and let fly, more in hope of frightening the

German away than of doing any real damage. The very first round disembowelled the enemy machine and blew it out of the air. As Wilson gawked in disbelief at the falling wreckage, the irrepressible Captain Armstrong whooped with delight and dubbed him "Sir Macro Wilson, Bart., Governor of the Leeward Isles".

Later, in his official report, Armstrong would drily note: "Yesterday was excellent for a new ship. At one moment we were sinking a merchant vessel with the after 4.7, covering the military with the foremost 4.7, engaging aircraft with a 4", and the close range weapons were covering the landing party against German snipers. Unfortunately there was no torpedo target."

Meanwhile, *Oribi* had moved up Ulvesund according to plan and at precisely 1000 put Captain Birney and his half troop ashore at Rodberg, a little village on the coastal road just south of North Vaagso. Their main task was to protect the north flank of the main landing by seeing that no reinforcements from the German battery at Halsoer (which was known to have an infantry support platoon attached, as did the one in the target area) got down to South Vaagso via the coastal road. Birney immediately dispatched a sizeable fighting patrol into North Vaagso to take out the telephone central and arrest the local quisling leader, Johan Setland. While this patrol was out the rest of the landing party set about preparing the demolition of the coastal road at a point where it ran along a narrow ledge hacked out of the mountainside.

Unbeknown to the "Archery" force, which had lost its long-range vision when the deck-to-air radio link failed, a small coastal convoy had just rounded the Stadtlandet and was bearing down on Vaagso Island from the north. Escorted by the armed trawler *Donner*, a sister to the gallant but ill-fated *Föhn*, this convoy had sailed out of Narvik several days earlier and was bound eventually for Rotterdam, picking its way carefully down the *Indreled* to avoid the omnipresent British submarines lurking in the dark waters of the North Sea.

The convoy split at the northern tip of the island. The armed tug *Rechtenfleth*, 200 tons, and the steamer *Anita L.M. Russ*, 2,800 tons, turned in and started down Ulvesund towards the cauldron around South Vaagso, their masters assuming apparently that the gunfire reverberating from the hillsides was some kind of coast defence exercise. But the steamer *Anhalt*, displacing some 5,930 tons, was far too large to negotiate the narrow passage between Maaloy and South Vaagso. She swung out to seaward to pass around the larger island, with *Donner* as escort. They would rejoin the convoy in Vaagsfjord—or so they thought.

Oribi, after putting Birney's men ashore, had moved back down the fjord to assist *Onslow* in dealing with the beached German vessels. The two destroyers had just finished demolishing *Fritzen* and *Föhn* when the first element of the new German convoy appeared, steaming innocently down upon the smoking harbour. The lookouts on all four vessels called out simultaneously, but the two German captains made the fatal error of mistaking the British destroyers for German warships. *Russ,* in the lead, carefully spelled out A-N-I-T-A L-M R-U-S-S on her blinker light. *Oribi*'s captain, Commander J. E. H. McBeath, realized immediately what was happening and instructed his yeoman of signals to reply slowly in kind. The range closed as the signal lamp on *Oribi*'s bridge began clattering.

There was absolutely no doubt in anyone's mind as to the precise moment when the Germans realized their mistake. Suddenly there was a wild flurry of signals on the bridges of both the oncoming vessels, the tug turned hard to port and the merchantman hard to starboard, and they both ran aground violently as *Oribi* opened fire. The German crews went over the rails—many of them were subsequently picked up and carried home as prisoners—and *Oribi,* unable to get away a boarding party because Birney's commandos had taken all her boats ashore, leisurely destroyed the two ships with gunfire.

Birney and his men had been too occupied on shore to pay much attention to the contretemps which befell the two German craft. The fighting patrol had collected the hapless Setland, blown up the telephone and telegraph office, and returned to the landing-point without difficulty. But now the Germans were pressing them.

The German battery at Halsoer had been paid a visit early in the morning by three Blenheims. According to plan, these aircraft made a great deal of noise and buzzed around at some length, but their bombs did no serious damage and when they finally left the German gunners crawled out of their shelters to hear what sounded like heavy gunfire in the south. The battery commander, Leutnant Lienkamp, listened puzzled for a few minutes and then went into his command post to ring through to South Vaagso, but of course no one answered because the Germans there were all busy fighting for their lives. Sebelin had already deployed his telephone orderlies on the firing line.

Lienkamp called back to headquarters of the 181st Division, which was responsible for the entire area, and asked what was going on. No one at division knew for sure, but it appeared that there was some kind of a British landing going on at South Vaagso; observers on Rugsundo had seen warships and landing craft approaching Maaloy before their vision was obscured by dense smoke in front of the apparent target. Lienkamp reported that he was not engaged and received rather vague instructions to send someone out and try to find out what was happening.

Since there was no sign of any attack impending around his own position, Lienkamp told his infantry platoon to patrol down the coastal road, determine the situation, and see what help the troops at Halsoer might lend in the events to the south. Hurrying through North Vaagso, this detachment discovered that British troops had already been in and out of the town, having just withdrawn southwards after destroying the communications facilities. The Germans followed cautiously, and a small contact patrol bumped one of the British outposts on the coastal road. A shooting match ensued, and one German was killed and another vanished, presumably captured by the British. The Halsoer platoon hurried in to engage and the pressure on Birney's beachhead mounted rapidly. So far the Number 2 Commando soldiers at Rodberg had taken no casualties, but the Germans were closing in and it was clear the position could not be held for long. British demolitionists blew the road, thereby completing the last of Group V's assigned tasks, while Birney got on the radio to ask for *Oribi* to come and bail him out.

Oribi was already on the way back, and appeared a few minutes later. Birney's men tumbled into their boats under fire and pulled energetically for the waiting warship while the Germans rushed forward into the abandoned British beachhead and showered them with small-arms fire. But this fusilade drew no blood, and *Oribi* immediately opened up with everything she had, suppressing the German fire. A moment later *Onslow* too steamed up from the south and the two destroyers hosed the German positions with hot steel while the commandos scrambled aboard and *Oribi*'s launches were hoisted back on to the davits.

Then *Onslow* and *Oribi* turned and moved off towards Maaloy and the burning town, where fighting was still in progress.

19

UNWANTED ATTENTIONS

Kenya was by far the largest and most obvious target in the fjord, and those on board had been having as busy a day as did the landing parties and the destroyer crews.

As the initial three landing parties stormed ashore at Hollevik, South Vaagso and Maaloy, the two troopships slid off to the north edge of the fjord where the huge shoulder of land just south of the town would shelter them from whatever reaction the attack might provoke from the Maaloy battery. The Hunt-class destroyer *Chiddingfold*, whose relatively light armament was of little use in coastal bombardment but offered a powerful defence against intruding enemy aircraft, crowded into Slaaken bay to help protect them; *Offa*, once the landing parties were safely ashore and her own part in the preliminary bombardment finished, moved out to her preassigned patrol station at the mouth of the fjord.

This left *Kenya* and (initially) *Onslow* and *Oribi* competing for the limited space just south of Maaloy. Standing on the bridge of any of the ships, one felt that he could, simply by stretching out his arms, touch both walls of the fjord at once. It was an uncomfortable feeling at best, and even the army passengers could sense the uneasiness of the seamen, accustomed to having miles of open sea room about them. It was an especially awkward situation for *Kenya*, as her ability to manoeuvre was further restricted by the requirements of the signallers, who needed to keep a clear line of sight to all shore parties to ensure visual contact. Visual signalling was particularly important as a link to Group II in South Vaagso, who had lost two Number 18 radio sets in getting ashore under fire from the German strongpoint and in the accidental bombing of one of their landing craft.

But at the same time *Kenya* had to keep up steerage way, to permit her to dodge the fire that came in from the Rugsundo battery and bombing attacks from German aircraft which penetrated the R.A.F.'s aerial umbrella.

The Rugsundo battery was a real thorn in *Kenya*'s side, firing intermittently throughout the day and keeping British nerves on edge. Having once been silenced during the initial bombardment, the German gunners came to life again shortly after 0930, when the smoke hanging over the southern reaches of the fjord began to thin out a bit. Everyone on the cruiser's bridge was watching the first flight of Blenheims arrive overhead, and the R.N.Z.A.F. liaison officer was trying to establish radio contact with them when shells began to splash into the quiet waters of the fjord. *Kenya* swung her "A" and "B" batteries around to engage, while the admiral ordered *Chiddingfold* to move rapidly across the front of the enemy battery, dropping additional smoke floats and reinforcing the dissipating smokescreen with funnel smoke. *Chiddingfold* hastened to comply, popping off a few salvoes from her own meagre armament as she came broadside to the enemy, and for a few minutes the roar of the naval guns drowned out the sounds of combat on shore. Then the German fire ceased once more, and the British guns fell silent.

The joint headquarters aboard the cruiser faced numerous command problems throughout the day, occasioned most often by the loss of contact with the two leading troops in South Vaagso. The headquarters was forever flashing visual messages to the command post on shore asking for situation reports, and Charley Head (who had not the faintest idea what was going on up forward because *he* had no reliable contact with the leading troops either, and could not locate the colonel who was somewhere up there with them) sent back encouraging replies, stating vaguely that the fighting was progressing well. Some of these messages got through by radio, but just as frequently they had to be repeated by visual means because the signalman could not read a particular word or phrase; when all the radio sets were in operation at once there was all sorts of interference and static crackling in the receivers situated in such close proximity to one another on a bridge festooned with jury aerials.

The problem was further complicated by the German air attacks which came in at intervals throughout the day. None of these attacks was in sufficient force to press in and do any real damage, but they were a constant source of harassment to Captain Denny who spent much of the day weaving his ship

about in the tightly restricted channel as the aircraft bore in. The
R.A.F. fighter umbrella lost several aircraft trying to fend off
these attacks, but still Denny was obliged to twist and wheel
Kenya about in the treacherous tidal currents, with shoal waters
on one hand and rocky cliffs on the other. Every time he moved
more than a few cable lengths westward down the main channel
the bulge of land south of the town would blank out communication with the shore parties, bringing groans from the frustrated
signallers.

There was a definite routine established for dealing with
bombing attacks. Everyone else on the bridge went about his
own business while the captain kept one eye cocked towards the
bombers making their runs overhead. Only when he saw a bomb
actually released would Denny call out "Take cover" and
instruct his helmsman to put the wheel hard over one way or the
other. At the captain's command, all business on the bridge came
to an instantaneous halt, everyone dropping prone on the deck
with his helmet over the back of his head and remaining
motionless until the bomb burst somewhere nearby and Denny
announced "All clear". Before the battle Major Henriques had
heard the Navy making arrangements for hot cocoa and soup to
be distributed to all hands at regular intervals, and had instructed
his own orderly to see that the Army did at least as well as the
Navy, with perhaps a spare cup now and then for the admiral and
the captain. Now as one of the German bombs whistled down
and Henriques and the brigadier lay with their noses pressed into
the steel deck plating, he noticed a pair of army boots standing
upright only a few feet before his eyes. He glanced up somewhat
sheepishly to find his batman, who had just emerged on to the
bridge with a tray of steaming cups, standing politely at attention
amidst all the prone senior officers. "Soup, sir," announced the
orderly in a bored tone as the bomb burst nearby.

From time to time *Kenya* hurled a few rounds into the
Rugsundo battery's position, partly to keep her guns ranged on
target as she moved about the fjord and partly to keep the
German gunners down. This last aim was not an unqualified
success, for although the battery remained silent most of the time
it developed an embarrassing habit of coming to life at inopportune moments, usually just when everyone on the cruiser was
busy worrying about some other problem. Again and again the
German gunners plunked rounds into the water alongside the
cruiser and, as we have already seen, eventually scored a clean

hit, exploding a round against *Kenya*'s armour belt above the waterline. Splinters flew through the boys' mess-deck but fortunately the compartment was empty so no one was hurt. A few minutes later another round from Rugsundo scored a near miss, spraying the exposed decks with shell fragments and wounding one seaman. Testy as a cow elephant in heat who finds herself stalked by an amorous mouse, *Kenya* lashed out again at the German gunners. Once more they were temporarily silenced, but never could the cruiser rid herself of their unwanted attentions.

After *Onslow* and *Oribi* disappeared into the smoke billowing across the Maaloy Strait, there was a lengthy period during which the admiral sought in vain to determine the situation just north of the little island. The captains of the destroyers were too fully occupied to take the time needed to draw up a comprehensive report; fragmentary messages poured in from them as fast as the yeomen on the cruiser's bridge could take them down:

> ONSLOW TO REAR-ADMIRAL CRUISER X ARMED TRAWL-
> ER AGROUND SOUTH OF KAPELNOES POINT.
> ORIBI TO REAR-ADMIRAL CRUISER X UNABLE COMPLY
> YOUR INSTRUCTIONS TO BOARD COASTAL STEAMER
> AGROUND SOUTH OF KAPELNOES POINT X ALL MY BOATS
> ASHORE WITH GROUP FIVE LANDING PARTY.

Admiral Burrough dealt with each message as it came in, turning to his Chief Yeoman of Signals and instructing him how to reply: "Make to *Onslow:* Board her." "Make to *Oribi:* Sink her." For all the excitement he showed, he might have been sorting peaches.

But no clear picture of the over-all situation emerged from this series of spot reports. Ulvesund still lay hidden behind a haze of smoke; events were developing faster than they could be reported in detail. Finally the admiral sent off *Kenya*'s motor launch, bearing an officer with instructions to assess the situation north of the island and report back. Lieutenant J. N. Kempton, R.N., drew this detail, taking with him as his companion one of *Kenya*'s "snotties", Midshipman Todd.[1] They chugged away

---

[1]The complement of midshipmen assigned to ships of the Royal Navy are traditionally known to the rest of the crew by this descriptive epithet. The lieutenant-commander responsible for their training, guidance and welfare is invariably christened "Snotties' Nurse".

and vanished into the blanket of smoke obscuring the strait, but no sooner did they emerge on the far side than the launch began drawing a great deal of fire from the alarmed Germans in the town, who mistook it for a landing craft presumably bearing a party trying to outflank them. In only a few minutes the boat was afire and Mr. Todd had been wounded in the leg; the craft blazed up like a torch and Kempton and Todd took to the water. The flaming derelict drifted slowly away on the current, leaving them in a critical situation, but a few moments later there was a low throb of engines and *Prince Leopold*'s support landing craft under command of sub-Lieutenant Snead, who had been directed to investigate the approaching motor launch, pulled alongside and fished the two men out of the chilly waters. The Germans in the town immediately turned their guns on the heavily-armed S.L.C. but it spit back angrily at them and churned away unharmed.

The day wore on. The sun, having peeped across the mountain-tops at last, now shone down upon the town itself, slid across the sky, and touched the hilltops behind the western shore. The shadows of the wharves and fjord-side buildings lengthened once more, poking dark fingers into Ulvesund. Buildings still blazed in the town, and gunfire resounded from the hillsides. Spot reports coming in from the shore parties were quickly marked up on the chart in the cruiser's flag plot.

At last the crisis seemed to have passed; a signal from Durnford-Slater advised the brigadier that German resistance was diminishing gradually, and demolition tasks were progressing rapidly. Already, sunset was growing near. And when the sun went down, full darkness would follow soon afterwards, even though the clock showed mid-afternoon. The naval and military commanders conferred briefly, and agreed that it was time to start withdrawing committed elements. The withdrawal order was flashed to the shore parties immediately.

20

MISSION COMPLETED

Group 1's attack had by this time reached the northern portion of the town. The sharp skirmish at the red warehouse had delayed the advance for about forty-five minutes, while the blazing fires in the western sector had similarly halted the troops moving up the inland side of the main road. But once these obstacles were passed the attack finally regained its original momentum. Parties of commandos moved quickly from building to building and fence to fence, finding fewer Germans in their way now. Those enemy soldiers who stood and fought were dealt with quickly and efficiently: a burst of fire to pin them down, a Mills bomb or two, and the attack moved on. But most of the remaining Germans withdrew before the British onslaught, taking up new positions around the youth hostel on the northern outskirts of the town.

Durnford-Slater moved forward again and overtook Peter Young, who had crossed his men over to the west side of the main road after leaving the red warehouse and was now pressing northward.

"Hullo, Peter, what's the situation?"

"We just ran into a gang of Norwegian civilians, sir, sheltering behind a house back there. They say there are still Germans in that brick building across the street." He gestured briefly towards the home of Olav Froysa, the town dentist. "We're trying to winkle them out."

Young took the colonel on a quick tour of the immediate area. Close at hand stood the Myrestrand home, which the pre-raid intelligence reports had listed as requisitioned by Major Schroeder, the German commandant, for his personal quarters. An automobile stood beside the building, and this aroused the interest of the two Englishmen. Young threw open the door and entered, but there was no sign of anyone inside. He began

Mills Bomb

searching from room to room and the colonel followed him up the stairs to the second floor.

In one of the rooms an elderly German lay in bed, gasping for breath. He was pale and emaciated, either terribly sick or critically hurt in the fighting, but still conscious. When he saw the two armed men in British uniforms enter the room he began to tremble with fear. Young looked at him suspiciously but Durnford-Slater, whose brusque manner hid a compassionate nature unsuspected by most of his acquaintances, said, "Let him be." They turned and went back down the stairs and out of the house, taking with them the official documents they had discovered in their search of the premises.

By this time the attack had swept past the Firda factory, the last of the major objectives for the commando demolitionists.

Durnford-Slater sent off a report to the brigadier, and almost immediately received a reply: withdraw and re-embark the landing force.

The advance came to a halt. Forward elements set up roadblocks against any German counter-attack from the north and sat waiting for instructions. The colonel met with his troop commanders.

"We'll pull back one troop at a time," he told them. "2 Troop with Clement will lead off, then 6 under Young and finally 1 with Bradley. Bill, get set to blow up the Firda factory immediately." He glanced at his watch. "It's now 1245. I want everyone on the way back by 1310. I'd better get back down to my command post. Peter, you're in charge up here." So saying, he hurried off to the rear, as jaunty looking as ever, if somewhat begrimed.

Hooper's men were already withdrawing and finding the process nearly as dangerous as had been the advance; a few bypassed snipers began to pop up here and there, taking snap shots at the British as they went by. Trooper Peachy spotted one lying doggo behind a mound of snow beside the road and quickly routed him out, the troop's last prisoner of the day.

Captain Bradley discovered that only one of his own men— Trooper Habron—was still with him, and that he had no demolitions in the forward area. What with the delay in advancing through the main part of the town the 1 Troop demolition parties under Lieutenant Etches, who had been wounded in the elbow shortly after landing but was still very much in action, were still busily occupied laying charges in the other factories to the south. If none of them caught up within the next ten or fifteen minutes some other means of dealing with the Firda factory would have to be found.

Young too took a hasty count and discovered that of the eighteen men who had come across from Maaloy with him he could now dispose of only Lance-Sergeant Herbert and five troopers. All the rest had been detailed to odd jobs along the way, guarding prisoners and helping wounded men back to the landing-point. For the first time he remembered Lance-Corporal Halls and Trooper Lewinton, whom he had posted in the upper window of the factory building overlooking the red warehouse with positive instructions to stay there until he sent for them. Were they still sitting there with their Bren gun? He turned to Trooper Hilton.

"Hilton, do you think you can find that building where we left Halls and Lewinton? Right, well, double back there and tell them to pull out. They may as well go straight back to the landing-place; we'll be starting off ourselves in a few minutes."

Trooper Hilton, who had never really taken commando training and was actually the troop clerk, had begged permission to take part in the raid and Captain Young finally consented, putting him under Sergeant Herbert whom he privately instructed to "keep an eye on Roger—he's never been shot at before". A military innocent who still preferred to think of himself as a commercial artist, Hilton had acquitted himself well enough during the day, although a certain element of luck seems to have been in his favour: after the fight at the red warehouse Captain Young sent him back for more grenades and in the flower of his innocence he eventually reappeared with two sacksful, wandering casually up the middle of the main street in a sector where every British soldier who put his nose out of cover had been forced to run a gauntlet of sniper fire; he was somewhat puzzled by all the people trying frantically to wave him into cover.

Now Hilton set off to find Halls and Lewinton, who at this moment were sitting idly in their window wondering whether Captain Young might have forgotten them entirely, completely unaware that a demolition party downstairs was preparing to blow the whole building out from under them. A few minutes later the building went up and Hilton arrived to find a smoking ruin. He had a few bad moments before he learned that by good fortune someone in the demolition party had thought to have a look upstairs before lighting the fuses; Halls and Lewinton had got out safely.

Meanwhile the colonel, coming back down the main street through the southern part of the town, found a small knot of British soldiers gathered around a mortally wounded German lying in the street. They were trying to give first aid to the enemy soldier, who had been hit in the chest and obviously had only minutes left to live; he could not be moved and was gasping with pain. Seeing Durnford-Slater approaching him, the man beckoned weakly and then, surprisingly, offered his hand. The colonel took the proffered hand and grasped it warmly—it was a highly emotional moment for him—and then went off about his business, feeling lightened by a soldier's benediction. It seemed to put the whole action in perspective, a good, hard fight with no quarter asked or given.

At the north end of the town Captain Young was sending off his men in small parties. Only a small rearguard remained with him now. Lacking explosives, Bill Bradley had managed to set the Firda factory afire; smoke poured out of the windows. In the final minutes someone brought in one last prisoner, a small, grubby-looking German in a huge greatcoat reaching almost to his ankles. Confronted with this Chaplinesque figure, so much the antithesis of the Aryan superman, Peter Young could not resist asking him in bad German, "Are *you* a Prussian?"

"*Nein, nein*," replied the prisoner in a shocked tone. "*Pommer!*"

At this all the British doubled up in helpless laughter while the puzzled Pomeranian peered owlishly at them, trying to fathom what manner of madmen he had fallen amongst.

By 1300 Young's little rearguard were the only British troops left in the northern half of the town, and were growing more and more aware of their vulnerability in event of a German counterattack; it would be downright embarrassing to get cut off from the landing-point at this stage of affairs. So Young decided to withdraw immediately, moving back slowly through the town, alert for bypassed snipers. The scruffy little Pomeranian, christened "Hermann" by his captors, was prodded to the head of the column and they moved along steadily. At each intersection or open area there was a call of "Vorwarts, Hermann!" and the prisoner moved out into the open first, followed by the Britishers. No one fired at them.

Further down the street they came upon two sandbags full of Mills bombs, and enlisted a pair of young Norwegians to carry these back to the landing-point. There was no point in leaving perfectly good ammunition to the enemy. Captain Young paused briefly to cut the epaulettes from the uniform of a dead German lying near the Hagen Hotel, and they moved on to the landing-place.

Most of the principal objectives of the raid had been achieved. The Maaloy battery had been completely wiped out; every man of the battery was dead or a prisoner, and the guns destroyed. The Firda factory was ablaze, and the other large factories already lay in ruins. The radio transmitter station was out of action, its tower crumpled to the ground. Across the fjord the remains of the main building of the Mortenes factory at Deknepol sent a pillar of smoke into the sky. The gutted ruins of an armed trawler and six sizeable steamers lay on the rocks along the banks of the fjord. The telephone exchanges were gone; German bodies lay here and there among the buildings of the town; the wharves and surrounding buildings had crumpled into the fjord. As the last British elements passed safely by, Lieutenant Etches, a sling supporting his wounded arm, fired the charges in the Seternes lighthouse, completely destroying the mechanism. Then he spread out his men to cover the reembarkation as planned.

A group of 1 Troop men were standing around the landing-place waiting to board the landing craft. Suddenly Lieutenant Pooley's web equipment burst into flame. Pooley dived into a snowbank, rolling over and over as he shed the burning belts. In the space of a few minutes the same thing happened to two other men; no one could explain the cause. Perhaps small bits of phosphorus had been wedged all this time in the weave of their webbing, and had only dried out as they withdrew through the heat of the blazing buildings.

Most of the landing craft were away now, and only the huge factory next to the landing-place, prepared for demolition by "Slinger" Martin and his men shortly after the landings, stood intact out of all the objectives listed before the raid. The colonel and Lieutenant Head were down at the beach supervising the loading of the last boats as Young's rearguard reported in with their prisoner.

Captain Martin decided the time had come, and ordered Sergeant Miller to fire the charges. Everyone took cover behind the nearest solid object while Miller entered the factory. There was a pause, a trill from Miller's police whistle (the signal that he was lighting the fuses), and then Miller galloped out the door and hurled himself down beside Martin, who had sought the cover of a huge rock. The earth shuddered and a giant shockwave rattled the helmet on every British head. Then the whole factory collapsed in a heap with the roof overhanging the water, smoke billowed skyward, and it began to snow—sardine tin labels. Martin's men had tamped the charges by packing boxes solidly around them, and the boxes they had chosen contained thousands of printed labels ready to be placed on the cans.

As Lieutenant Etches's rearguard withdrew to the beach there was a gentle throbbing sound which gradually grew louder. *Onslow* and *Oribi* appeared through the smoke, a stirring sight seen at close range by watchers on the beach. The two ships slipped quietly and purposefully out of the Maaloy strait into the

main fjord, reminding Martin of a pair of lions slinking home
from a successful hunt. Figures could be seen walking about the
decks and the chugging of the destroyers' engines was clearly
audible as the wash from their propellers gently rocked the
landing craft still nosed into the beach.

Then only one boat was left on the shore and only two men
in British uniform stood on Norwegian soil: the colonel and his
friend Charley Head, each of whom wanted to be last man off.
"Go on, get in," said Durnford-Slater in his most official tone.
Head grinned guiltily like a small boy caught with his hand in
the jam pot, and complied. The colonel leaped aboard and as the
boat backed away from the shore he sent a brief radio message to
Brigadier Haydon on the flagship: ALL TROOPS REEMBARKED X PRO-
CEEDING PRINCE CHARLES X DURNFORD-SLATER

As the last landing craft ploughed back across the millpond
waters of the fjord, three rifle shots cracked out from somewhere
north of the landing-place. It was the only sign that any Germans
had been left alive.

21

PARTING SHOTS

But the day's action had not ended yet. As the landing craft
growled away from the shore into the quiet waters of the fjord
the sound of heavy gunfire echoed from the direction of the open
sea at the fjord entrance. *Offa*, which had been dutifully patrolling the entrance all day while her sister ships were happily
shooting up German vessels inside the Inner Leads, had found a
target at last.

To be more accurate, there were two targets. The unlucky
recipients of *Offa*'s attentions were the remaining vessels of the
coastal convoy which had split up earlier at the northern end of
the island after an uneventful passage around the Stadtlandet
peninsula. While *Anita L.M. Russ* and *Rechtenfleth* blundered
innocently into the middle of the party in progress in Ulvesund
the larger steamer *Anhalt* and her escort, the armed trawler

Donner, steamed placidly down the outer shore of the island, their crews blissfully unaware of the dramatic events taking place only a few air miles away across the mountainous spine of the island. A few minutes after noon, as they rounded the southwestern bulge of the island, they were sighted by lookouts on *Offa* and their size, course and estimated speed were flashed to the flagship. An immediate reply from Admiral Burrough directed Commander R. A. Ewing, *Offa*'s master, to capture the enemy vessels if practicable. A second signal flashing from the flagship sent *Chiddingfold* churning towards the entrance at flank speed to lend a hand.

At 1220, as *Anhalt* swung her bows around towards the fjord entrance, German lookouts caught their first glimpse of the two British destroyers coursing out to intercept. *Anhalt*'s captain reacted quickly: just as the British guns opened fire he put his helm all the way over to port and ran straight in for the shore, beaching his vessel just off Baadsundshalsen Point in the fjord entrance. Then he and his crew took to their lifeboats. *Chiddingfold* hove to abeam of the beached vessel. Meanwhile, *Donner* turned out to sea and ran for her life, with *Offa* in hot pursuit.

It was as uneven a contest as had been the brief engagement between *Föhn* and *Offa*'s two sister ships in Ulvesund. *Donner*'s crew were every bit as bellicose as had been *Föhn*'s, but being in the unfortunate position of quarry in a stern chase they could bring only one small gun to bear on their pursuer, which opened fire from one thousand yards with the four-inch gun mounted in the foredeck turret. British shells smacked into the trawler with deadly effect. Suddenly *Donner* caught fire, the diesel oil tanks blazing up fiercely; her crewmen leapt over the rail into the water, leaving the abandoned vessel steaming steadily out to sea at ten knots. *Offa* did not even slow down as she raced by the Germans bobbing in the water, merely dropping them a few Carley floats in passing. Ewing was still intent on bringing home a prize.

In a short time the destroyer overhauled the smoking derelict, and with some difficulty the helmsman laid her close alongside while a boarding party leapt across the gap, under orders to stop the engines on the German craft. But the blazing fire below-decks blocked access to the engine-room, so *Offa* again pulled close abeam and passed fire-hoses to the boarding party, who played them into the engine-room to bring the fire under control.

After that they succeeded in getting the screws stopped, and made a thorough search of the prize.

So out of all the German vessels encountered, harried and pursued by the British destroyers that day, one only had been captured more or less intact. But now Ewing too found that the fates seemed to be against him: the prize crew reported that they were unable to start the engines. The fire-hoses had not only flooded out the fire but also flooded the air intakes; additionally, there was not enough diesel fuel left on board to sail the vessel home even if the engines *could* be started.

Ewing knew that taking his prize in tow was out of the question, for at all costs the British vessels must move fast and get out of range of Norwegian-based Luftwaffe aircraft before the following morning, and one does not tow a derelict vessel at high speeds in the North Sea. Disgusted, he had the German vessel's two Oerlikons and one Maxim gun transferred on board *Offa,* and ordered the boarding party to scuttle their prize. This done, *Offa* swung around and started back to search for the crewmen in the water.

Meanwhile, *Chiddingfold* had closed on the beached *Anhalt* in time to see the captain and crew pulling for shore in their lifeboats. A German-speaking British seaman took over the loudspeaker and ordered the men in the boats to come alongside the destroyer or be fired upon. The only reaction from the boats was a frantic redoubling of the oarsmen's efforts to reach the shore, now only a few yards away. *Chiddingfold* opened fire, sinking one of the two boats immediately, but just then a flight of Heinkel 111s appeared overhead, drawing all attention skyward; as the destroyer swung her guns up to take the aircraft under fire the second lifeboat reached shore and *Anhalt*'s captain escaped with half his crew.

The German aircraft paid the target area a brief visit and then departed. *Chiddingfold* lay off the shore and began systematically pounding the beached steamer, making sure that the survivng crew members would find her damaged beyond repair upon their return.

Back in the fjord *Kenya* was flaying the Rugsundo battery again. The German fire ceased and *Onslow* and *Oribi,* emerging from the Maaloy strait, laid more smoke to mask the battery position during the withdrawal from the fjord.

The last landing craft was hoisted aboard *Prince Charles*

and Commander Fell flashed a message to the flagship. Official sunset was only three minutes away, but the sun had long since disappeared behind the hills to the west and dusk was gathering over the fjord. Admiral Burrough gave the signal for the ships to get under way.

Durnford-Slater joined Commander Fell on *Prince Charles*'s bridge. To Fell, he looked the personification of the public image of the commandos: smoke-blackened and begrimed, his tunic burnt and blood from his injured hand smeared on his clothing, pistol still clutched in his hand, and three grenades nestling atop the ''Mae West'' still blown up hard beneath his tunic, but grinning happily. The colonel was obviously pleased with the day's work.

They stood together and watched as the ships in the fjord swung ponderously around in the tricky tidal current, pointed their prows to the open sea and slipped out of the fjord, filing one by one past the hulk of *Anhalt* lying battered on the rocks. As they went past, *Onslow* and *Oribi* each pumped a few more rounds into the wreckage in parting salute.

22

TRIUMPHANT RETURN

Daylight faded as the Norwegian coast fell astern. The main goal in everyone's mind now was to put as much distance as possible between themselves and that coast by dawn, for first light of the new day would undoubtedly bring the Luftwaffe out in force, bent on vengeance. Beaufighters of the aerial umbrella still circled overhead, but this was the last scheduled sortie; when these aircraft went home, the ships would be on their own as far as air defence was concerned.

''It was dusk,'' Brigadier Haydon recalled afterwards, ''and shortly we would be screened by the welcome darkness. The admiral had issued the most stringent instructions to all ships that, in order to avoid giving any indication to German aircraft of where we were or what course we were following, no smoke whatsoever was to be made.

"Suddenly, however, just before darkness fell, there came from one of the escorting destroyers a great belch of the blackest, oiliest smoke imaginable.

"The admiral watched it rise slowly into the air and hang there—a menacing beacon to all Germans with eyes to see. Then, without raising his voice, he said: 'Make a signal to that captain from me—"What's cooking?" ' It was a far more effective means of dealing with the incident than any formal reproof would have been."

Aboard the transports, the troops were jubilant—and hungry. In the excitement of the day's events few had had a chance to eat the haversack rations issued them that morning aboard ship, and owing to the great storm on the way over no one had had a hot meal since Boxing Day. The troop compartments echoed to a chorus of gurgling stomachs, but the ships' galley cooks were still very much occupied at their action stations, helping the surgeons care for the wounded. It was catch-as-catch-can for the evening meal. On board *Prince Leopold,* Temporary Paymaster-Lieutenant J. Grogan took off his coat and, with the help of a handful of commando volunteers, managed to get the galley fires going and put together a hot meal of sorts for all hands.

The German prisoners were locked in one of the troop lavatories on board *Prince Leopold*. From time to time they were paraded on deck for a bit of air, then locked away again in their improvised quarters. The War Office intelligence specialists who had come along on the raid had the Germans out one by one, interrogating them on a bewildering variety of subjects: coastal defences in Norway, organization of their unit, news from the home front, current policies of the occupation forces, latest rumours circulating in the area, their own backgrounds and military specialities.

On the four ships carrying elements of the landing force, officers made a hurried nose-count and came up with the surprising news that every commando who had splashed ashore that morning was positively accounted for, either back aboard ship or known dead on shore. The German intelligence services would have no prisoners of their own to interrogate, and would have a difficult time piecing together the story of what had happened in

He 111

the area: too many of their own men were killed or captured. Not a German had been left alive on Maaloy.

In the sick-bays doctors and attendants treated the wounded. The only priority recognized was the urgency of a man's wound awaiting medical attention; wounded men have no nationality. Lieutenant O'Flaherty had already undergone the first of a series of operations that would stretch out over the next two years; his eye was gone, but he would fight again in time. Major Churchill, surprisingly, had come off Maaloy on a stretcher even though uninjured in the actual fighting. Once the island was secured he set about searching some buildings for documents and a demolitionist thoughtlessly blew down a wall he happened to be leaning against, injuring him painfully but, as it developed, not seriously.

The last vestiges of daylight shrunk closer to the horizon. Three Heinkel 111s escorted by two Me–109s droned out after the fleeing formation of ships, but ran into a wall of fire as every anti-aircraft weapon in the formation opened up. The German aircraft broke formation and veered away, and then were set upon by the four Beaufighters of the final R.A.F. sortie, which knocked down two of the Heinkels. The rest of the Germans ran for home and the four Beaufighters joined up to pass once over the fleet, dipping their wings in salute, and disappear into the western sky. Overhead, the last faint orange glow of sunset shrivelled and died. A bright quarter moon hung in the sky as night fell over the task force.

"Slinger" Martin made his way down to his assigned cabin after seeing to the storage of unused ammunition. Two sailors armed with rifles stood guard outside the door of an adjacent compartment. Martin asked who was inside.

" 'Ave a look, mate," grinned one of the sailors, throwing open the door. Two fair-haired young women, loosely clad in over-sized pyjamas belonging to the ship's doctor, whose quarters they were occupying, glanced up as the door opened. They were the "comfort girls" who had been captured in the German billets.

"Jerry floozies," confided the sailor with a wink as he shut the door. "Yer can't keep 'em down. Me an' my mate 'ere 'ave been 'avin' 'eart attacks!"

A little later Martin had occasion to emerge once more from his own cabin on some errand. Outside the adjacent door two rifles with fixed bayonets leaned against the bulkhead. There was no sign of any sailors.

A quiet burial service was read on board *Prince Charles* and the bodies of three commandos—Captain Giles, whose grieving troops had refused to leave him to be buried by the Germans, and two critically wounded men who died while undergoing treatment in the ship's sick-bay—were committed to the deep. Counting these and two other soldiers who died on board *Prince Leopold,* Number 3 Commando's total losses for the day's action were two officers and eleven other ranks killed outright, four other ranks died of wounds, and six officers and forty-seven other ranks wounded.

The Norwegians had lost Captain Linge killed and two other ranks wounded. All in all, 73 of the 525 men of the landing force had become casualties of some kind, or about 14 per cent. This is not by any means a heavy figure for so daring an operation, and was in fact considerably lower than had been anticipated in planning the raid.

As the Norwegian coast fell farther and farther behind and the men who had entered so tensely into action that same morning began to realize that they had got away with it and come

away safely, the curious lethargy which overtakes troops after a
violent engagement began to settle over the ships. Where the
men had been noisily elated at their success upon return to the
ships, excess adrenalin still pumpling through their veins, now
the emotional strain of the day's activities began to catch up and
one by one they fell silent, their nervous energies depleted.
Strained nerves suddenly went completely slack, and an air of
depression set in. Brigadier Haydon and Major Henriques, already turning their attention to the next scheduled operation for
the brigade—another attempt at Floro—suddenly found themselves wondering how they could possibly go through all this
again. When a coded radio message reported that a new gun
position had been positively identified, very close to the target,
Henriques suggested that the whole operation might better be
cancelled. The brigadier agreed immediately.

Weary troopers collapsed into their bunks without undressing.
For some, sleep was slow in coming despite their fatigue; they
lay silently smoking their cigarettes and listening to the humming
and creaking sounds of shipboard life, pondering the odd chances
which had brought them safely through the day while messmates
fell beside them.

Shortly after 1700, as the ships were proceeding in bright
moonlight, the air alarm sounded again. Another German aircraft
was approaching from astern, easily following the convoy's
wake gleaming on the sea. Once more the ships put up a "blind
barrage"[1] but the German bomber bored in and dropped a stick
of bombs so close across *Prince Charles*'s bow that the whole
ship shuddered and reverberated. Then the German wheeled and
disappeared into the darkness. The concussion of the near-miss
seriously damaged one of the ship's boilers and Commander Fell
had to order it shut down, reducing the vessel's speed drastically.
The other ships churned along at half-speed, keeping pace with
the limping transport, while the destroyers drew in closer for
protection.

Throughout the following day the force steamed slowly
home. No more German aircraft appeared, and as they entered
home waters Coastal Command Beaufighters began to appear
again, circling protectively overhead.

At 1800 hours on 28th December, the "Archery" force

---

[1] A wall of fire not directed at any specific target, usually used when the target's
exact position cannot be determined.

Bristol Beaufighter

steamed triumphantly into Scapa Flow. A hospital ship came alongside and took off the more serious casualties and Admiral Tovey, the "patron" of the whole operation, visited the ships briefly, stopping to confer with the admiral, the brigadier, Durnford-Slater and the master of each of the ships. A message of admiration from *Kenya*'s entire crew was read to the men of Number 3 Commando, and Durnford-Slater took the opportunity to have a few words with them himself. He was concerned that, having been "blooded" and enjoyed a notable success in their first major action, some of the men might tend to let down a little and let the fine edge wear away through negligence, so after complimenting them on their success he put on a stern face and gave them a warning:

"Future operations must be regarded as highlights in our lives. A very few of you didn't like the Vaagso operation and must leave the unit forthwith. Your behaviour and turnout must be irreproachable at all times. Have all the fun that's going— drinking, gambling, chasing the girls, and so on—if it appeals to you; but if these things interfere with your work they must be put aside. Personally, I have long, quiet periods without any of these diversions and recommend you do the same. You must always behave and look like super-soldiers. If you cannot, then there is no place for you in Number 3 Commando."

First news of the operation, a brief communiqué based on the admiral's signal that the operation was successfully completed, had already been flashed to the world. The force rode at anchor throughout the night and the next day while supplementary reports were phoned back to Whitehall, couriers came and went, and shipfitters came aboard to make good the more serious damages. Ralph Walling of Reuters, who had landed on Maaloy with Jack Churchill, went ashore to file a detailed story of the raid, which appeared on front pages throughout the free world the following morning.

At 2000 hours on the 29th the troopships finally weighed anchor and sailed for Invergordon to discharge troops, arriving there early the next morning. But someone had blundered: the expected trains were not waiting at pierside to take Number 3 Commando back to Largs. The men spent the day waiting impatiently aboard ship, while officers made furious phone calls. Finally, late that night, two special trains arrived and the weary soldiers were allowed to debark. The first train left as soon as it was loaded, but the second lay alongside the ship taking on ammunition and equipment until four in the morning. But at last it too pulled out of the dockyard, and on midafternoon of New Year's Eve Durnford-Slater arrived at Largs with the final contingent of his men. Among the mail and messages awaiting the colonel's attention was a notice that he had been awarded a Mention in Despatches for Operation "Claymore", that expedition to the Lofotens which now seemed like ancient history.

The party that took place in Largs that night was loud and memorable as Number 3 Commando welcomed 1942 in suitable fashion. But the joy was not entirely unrestrained; the next afternoon the colonel's landlady, bringing tea to his room, found him dejectedly staring at the Commando's casualty list, and thought that she saw tears in his eyes.

23

RUFFLED ALLY

On the 12th January the exiled King Haakon VII received about 250 of his subjects at Grosvenor House in London. Most of them were products of the recent "Archery" and "Anklet" operations, civilians who had begged a ride back to England with the raiding forces in order to join the Free Norwegian Armed Forces. Many of the young men had brought their families out with them, and about seventy of those present were children who gazed awestruck at the huge illuminated Christmas tree laden with presents from their king.

After a singing of patriotic songs the king made a short speech. "Your countrymen here in England," he said, "have not worked in vain for Norway's cause. Every successful operation brings the day of victory that much closer. In the end we cannot fail to drive the invaders from our homeland."

But the king's words concealed an underlying tension between Norway and her allies, a sore spot that had been further aggravated by the British attacks at Vaagso and in the Lofotens.

The Norwegian government-in-exile had never really endorsed pinprick thrusts of this sort, feeling that such minor operations did very little to hasten the end of the war but did invite retribution upon a captive populace. The relative advantages and disadvantages of an offensive policy had been debated at great length, but thus far the two governments had been unable fully to reconcile their positions. The British were determined that they must continue to cultivate the offensive spirit in their troops and keep up morale on the home front by conducting frequent raids, regardless of strategic gain or the lack of it; the Norwegians on the other hand were equally determined that raids into Norway should be permitted only when they stood to achieve some clear-cut and longstanding betterment of the strategic position.

British and Norwegian intelligence agencies worked in close co-operation and it was normal for the British to advise their counterparts that an operation was being prepared against a given target. But the tactical details were generally withheld, not from any special desire to keep the Norwegian government in the dark but simply because it is in keeping with established principles of military security to limit the number of persons having detailed knowledge of projected operations, the governing factor being the individual's actual need to know the details of the plan in order to carry out his own role in supporting it. The general concept of a strike against the German coast defences in the Vaagso area had been presented to the Norwegian authorities beforehand, and Martin Linge and some of his officers knew generally what was involved before they left London; but it made no more sense to the British to pre-brief these men in detail than it did to pre-brief their own troops. The final bits of information were withheld until everyone concerned was safely isolated aboard ship.

It is understandable, then, that the official British communiqué announcing the operational success at Vaagso failed to arouse any great enthusiasm among the Norwegian ministers in London, who quickly identified it as just another pinprick to goad the occupation forces into a greater fury. They immediately demanded a "meeting of the minds" with the British on the subject of future combined operations. If some solution could not be found, they hinted, the Norwegian government might well be forced to take a step everyone wished to avoid: public denunciation of the allied raids, which would of course drive a fatal wedge into the carefully-preserved façade of allied unity.

The task of soothing England's ruffled ally devolved upon Admiral Mountbatten, who reasoned that the logical first step was to acquaint Prime Minister Nygaardsvold and his cabinet with the positive gains achieved in such raids. As he himself was at the time engaged in another project of commensurate urgency, he despatched as his personal representatives his flag-captain and adjutant to deliver a carefully prepared briefing to the Nygaardsvold government, underlining the brilliant military success of the "Archery" sortie.

It was an unfortunate occasion from the British standpoint. The Combined Operations briefers arrived wearing an air of insuperable enthusiasm for the project, giving the impression that they were quite ready—nay, eager—to launch more strikes of a similar nature into occupied Norway. They came armed with statistics relating the light casualties sustained by the landing force to the disproportionately high ones believed to have been inflicted upon the enemy, with dramatic photographs showing British and Norwegian soldiers pressing forward before a background of blazing buildings, and with an impressive list of damages done to the enemy war effort: one complete coastal battery destroyed and another badly damaged, the enemy radio transmitter at Seternes completely wrecked, tons of shipping sent to the bottom or shot to pieces, and left rusting on the beach, wanted collaborators arrested and brought back to England for trial by their own sovereign, fish-oil factories demolished, lighthouses out of action, Germans taken prisoner. Surely no one could deny that the raid had cost the enemy dearly.

When they were done with their presentation Mr. Nygaardsvold himself rose to reply. Having lived for some years in the United States he could when he wished speak excellent English, but so upset was he now by the British argument that his remarks came forth in the expressive speech of his native land, addressed as much to his own ministers as to the British spokesmen.

Who could be so blind, he asked, as to delude himself that this effort could have done anything to shorten the ordeal of captive Norway? Undoubtedly the enemy had been annoyed by the very impudence of the operation lancing deep into the shoreline he sought to secure, but it could have only one result: the Germans would now strengthen their defences, making the ultimate victory even harder to achieve than it would have been if the raid had never taken place.

Meanwhile, what was the cost to Norway in terms of immediate loss? *Kompani Linge* had taken three casualties, one of them being its commanding officer. But the counting of Norway's losses could not stop there. What of the civil population? How many innocent civilians had died as the fighting raged around their homes? How many of those homes had been destroyed?

Further, any reckoning must include the continuing cost to the populace in the days to come. After the residents of the Lofoten Islands openly welcomed the "Claymore" landing force in March of that same year the Germans had sought to teach them a lesson by burning seventy homes to the ground. Who was prepared to say how many more homes were burning in Vaagso at this very minute, how many citizens being arrested and shipped off to concentration camps or, worse yet, summarily executed in the streets of their town? When all these costs were taken together, what lasting gain could be set to counterbalance them in the accounting book of war? Pointless raids into Norway would have to stop.

The elderly Prime Minister's angry talk went on for fifteen minutes, and the two British representatives did not need to wait a translation to sense the deep emotion with which he spoke. Clearly their own government had underestimated the strength of the Norwegians' objections to the raids. They withdrew from the meeting as tactfully as possible, voicing to Mr.

Nygaardsvold their promise to set his government's views accu
rately before their superiors.

This unhappy meeting marked an important milestone fo
both governments. The Norwegian government-in-exile bega
soon afterwards to organize its *Forsvarets Overkommando* (Arme
Services Joint Command) under Major-General Wilhelm Hansteen
one of whose avowed missions was to establish tighter co
ordination with the British inter-service agencies and give th
Norwegian government an organ of its own able to play a
effective part in planning operations in Norway. The British, fo
their own part, tacitly accepted the Norwegian view that an
future operations must have goals of such indisputable strategi
concern that the possible impact upon the civil population coul
be counted worthwhile; there would be no more harassment o
the German occupation forces for harassment's sake alone
Never again did a raid on the scale of the Vaagso enterpris
touch the Norwegian coast, although a few smaller operation
did go in, with a very vital objective indeed: bringing Germany'
attempt at the development of nuclear weapons to a halt.[1]

It marked a turning point of sorts for *Kompani Linge,* too
Never again after Vaagso would the Lingemen splash ashore i
uniform and shoot their way into a surprised German garrison
Instead, as *Forsvarets Overkommando* gradually assumed th
burden for the planning and conduct of operations in Norway, th
company was transformed and retrained to become the nucleu
of the force of skilled intelligence agents and saboteurs wh
slipped surreptitiously back into their homeland by ones an
twos. Their contribution there to the over-all war effort becam
one of the most brilliant chapters in the saga of allied operation
in Europe.

---

[1] The German experiments were completely dependent upon a supply of deuteriun
oxide ("heavy water"), produced in only one place in all Europe—the huge hydro
electric plant at Rjukan, in the Telemark district of Norway. A brilliant joint effort by th
Norwegians and the British, in which *Kompani Linge* played the leading role, succeede
in destroying the plant's production capacity as well as all existing stocks of the com
pound, and Germany never got the bomb. The complete story of this operation is vividl
recounted in *ASSAULT IN NORWAY* by Thomas Gallagher, another volume in Th
Bantam War Book series.

24

AFTERMATH IN NORWAY

But the story of the Vaagso attack does not end with the return of the raiding force to England and the bitter recriminations between the British and Norwegian governments. As the members of the "Archery" force dispersed to their home stations and the diplomats began to squabble, as the wounded lay in their hospital beds and telegrams were delivered to the relatives of the dead, a chain of circumstances had already been set in motion in Norway which would have a totally unexpected effect upon the future course of the war. Had Prime Minister Nygaardsvold known of the deliberations then taking place in occupied Europe as a direct result of the raid he might well have withdrawn his objections, for in the end the strategic consequences of this one pinprick thrust would be staggeringly disproportionate to the number of men and ships that sailed across the storm-whipped sea to Vaagso.

The raiding force had scarcely withdrawn from the fjord when German reinforcements began arriving upon the scene. Two full companies arrived by boat from Bergen, prudently waiting for the British destroyers to disappear over the horizon before approaching the mouth of the fjord. Even less welcome to the inhabitants was a twenty-seven man Gestapo detachment led by an unpleasant *untersturmfuhrer* named Tomas who scowled into town and immediately began asking sharp questions about just how much co-operation the landing force had received from local citizens.

Sizeable portions of the town lay in ruins. In addition to the factories destroyed according to the original plan drawn up at Combined Operations Headquarters, six large buildings used for commercial fishing enterprises, both hotels (including the annexe and store at Hagen's) and twenty private homes had burnt to the ground. Citizens milled around the wreckage trying to bring the fires under control and prevent damage to adjacent structures, while the surviving Germans collected themselves and began trying to count their own losses.

The damages to private property totalled over 5,000,000 kroner, but in terms of life and limb the civil population had come off remarkably well. During the fight around one of the beached German trawlers in Ulvesund a shell splinter killed assistant lighthouse keeper Ragnvald Torheim, but—surprisingly enough—not a single Norwegian civilian had been killed in the town proper, despite the fact that more than a hundred of them were caught up in the violent street fighting and forced to seek whatever cover they could find. Five citizens had been injured, none critically. But dead men in the uniforms of both sides lay scattered about the area and the Germans deputized a number of young Norwegians to assist in the gruesome task of collecting the bodies. The uniform pockets of the British dead were turned out but revealed nothing of intelligence interest; the withdrawing landing force, whose members had been warned against carrying official or personal documents into action, had taken the extra precaution of searching its own dead and removing everything but identity tags.

By the morning of the 28th some sort of picture of the German losses was beginning to take shape. The commanding general of the 181st Division, Generalmajor Kurt Woytasch, arrived to interview participants and survey the damage. In his official report he noted that the infantry in South Vaagso had lost eleven dead and seven wounded plus sixteen more men missing in action, presumably captured. Eleven German bodies had been found on Maaloy and thirty-five men were missing there. Some of these must also be presumed dead; witnesses told Woytasch that they had seen human figures blown right off the island in the fury of the opening bombardment. The German marine detachment had lost six men, and the Halsoer battery reported one soldier wounded and another missing in the engagement at Rodberg. A twenty-five-man detachment that had been in South Vaagso to pass the holidays was still trying to get an accurate accounting of its personnel; Sebelin had thrown these men into the line wherever needed. Losses among the crews of the beached and sunken ships had still not been determined. Surprisingly, the Rugsundo battery had lost only one man killed and eight wounded, despite being violently bombed and shelled at intervals throughout the day. With only two old Russian

13–cm guns, one of which was nonoperational through much of the action, the Germans on Rugsundo had given a very good account of themselves.

Woytasch asked specifically about secret documents and could turn up no positive proof that any had been lost, *Föhn*'s code books having presumably been destroyed. Still, as he reflected in his report, one must reckon with the possibility—a warning which unfortunately went unheeded, allowing the British to use the captured recognition signals and call letters to bluff their way into St. Nazaire harbour three months later in the first critical moments of the most brilliant and audacious raid in the history of the war, a raid which might well have been a failure had the German high command heeded Woytasch's warning and changed the codes currently in use.

Two things, though, were immediately apparent to the Germans: the raiding force had based its plan upon accurate detailed information of the target area, and such information could only have been collected with the co-operation of one or more local residents. Somehow, someone had passed intelligence to the British long before the raid took place. The Gestapo detachment began asking a lot of questions in an effort to determine who that someone might be.

Nearly seventy townspeople seemed to have left with the landing force, and the possibility existed that the agent or agents had fled by this expedient means. Still, the British intelligence service is noted for its thoroughness and would probably be reluctant to leave the area entirely uncovered, so perhaps something might yet turn up.

The investigation developed no really credible information pointing at any specific persons, but the Germans were not satisfied. Two respected local citizens, a school teacher named Ingebrigt Maurstad from North Vaagso and a local merchant, Bjorn Lem, from South Vaagso, were taken hostage for the safety of the captured *Nasjonal Samling* functionaries. Headquarters in Oslo decreed that the nearest male relative of each of the Norwegians who escaped to England with the "Anklet" and "Archery" forces should be arrested and shipped to the concentration camp at Grini. In practice this did not always work out. The population managed so to confuse the accounts of who was where (and when) that in the end the Germans were able to identify positively only sixty of the escapees from South Vaagso. For example, the town baker, questioned about the whereabouts of his son who had escaped to England, pointed tearfully to the body of the German he and O'Flaherty had left dying in the blazing house. The corpse was charred beyond recognition, all its clothing burnt away. The Germans accepted the baker's explanation that his son had been burned to death in the fighting, and the baker and his family went into mourning. The son trained as a flyer in Canada and later saw combat against the Germans while the father, wearing a black armband, went on baking bread for the residents of South Vaagso.

The Germans never succeeded in piecing together the full story of what had happened. Their efforts were frustrated by the fact that the Maaloy battery had taken a hundred per cent casualties, leaving no one to tell what actually took place on the island, and by the lack of a British prisoner who might be forced to reveal the other side of the story. Walking over the ground the next day, looking at the wreckage of the guns, the cuts in the protective wire entanglements and the places where bodies had been found, General Woytasch concluded that there had "probably" been some hand-to-hand combat around the guns, especially since some cartridge cases of both British and German manufacture were found in one of the gun pits. Stabsfeldwebel Passow, who had watched the initial bombardment of the island from the South Vaagso strongpoint, insisted that the Number 1 gun had got off at least one round before being dismounted by British shells, but then a heavy curtain of smoke obscured the island, shutting off his view. An observer on Rugsundo, peering through a rift in the smoke with his field glasses, had caught a glimpse of landing craft crawling across the surface of the fjord towards the tiny island, but what happened when they arrived there was to remain a melancholy mystery to the Germans until after the war.

At the South Vaagso strongpoint the German infantrymen had by extreme good fortune been working around their positions when the first rounds were fired, and thus were able to man their weapons with little delay. But still it was difficult to piece together just what had happened. Major Schroeder had been among the first casualties, wounded by a shellburst and carried off to his quarters where he was later visited by Durnford-Slater before he died. The commander of the infantry security company, Oberleutnant Bremer, was left in command of this critical area but a few minutes later he too went down, killed by an unidentified commando of 3 Troop, whereupon command devolved upon the two senior non-commissioned officers, Lebrenz and Passow.

Thus within an hour of the initial landing the fighting in the south end of town became an N.C.O.s' war; five of the six officers leading the two commando troops assaulting this sector became casualties, as did all their German counterparts. The battle broke up into a series of small violent skirmishes between desperate men in khaki and grey, slipping and skidding across snow-covered backyards to fire sub-machine guns and hurl grenades at one another, and to be shot down in turn by other men firing from windows and doorways of houses whose regular occupants trembled in whatever shelters they could find, wincing at each new explosion and crash of glass over their heads. The German strongpoint, sited to give covering fire across the front of the Maaloy battery against just such a contingency as had presented itself on the island, could not long resist the onslaught of the determined commandos, unleashed under cover of a withering fire from three warships in the nearby fjord. Bit by bit the Germans gave ground, withdrawing gradually into the southern sector of the town where Sebelin's patchwork force of clerks, orderlies and sailors was trying to set up a new line. Sebelin did yeoman service, rallying every man he could locate, be he army, navy, marine or merchant seaman, and disposing them in houses and sheds to block the British advance; the skill and determination with which his men did their duty is attested by the casualty list of the assault troops who attempted to break through the improvised strongpoints at the Ulvesund and Hagen hotels and the Steamship Wharf. But it was all very confused at the time, noisy and violent, and no one could say later exactly where he had been at any given time or even what route he had followed in the initial fighting.

Early in the day the first flash message of fighting around Vaagso reached General Falkenhorst, over-all commander of German forces in Norway, at his headquarters in Oslo, but it was fairly late before any real information got through. It was difficult for Falkenhorst to evaluate the situation, for at the same time he was receiving similar reports on the "Anklet" thrust into the Lofotens and calls from German naval headquarters in Norway to warn him that major elements of the British fleet were approaching the Norwegian coast at various points; German patrol aircraft had detected the Home Fleet's diversionary manoeuvre in the North Sea and were sending in position reports.

Details were still lacking at suppertime, but Falkenhorst sent news of the attack to Berlin in his regular evening bulletin

Number 367, stating that the enemy had apparently withdrawn.
There were, however, confusing reports that the Halsoer battery
was fighting against enemy ground forces an hour after the
British vessels had withdrawn from the fjord. Probably, as so
often happens in wartime, there was some kind of communications mix-up, but the end result was to further blur the situation.

Forty-eight hours after the raid South Vaagso was fairly
crawling with German troops. The town was put under martial
law and a curfew imposed, first from six in the evening until
eight in the morning, then later (after passions had cooled
somewhat and jangled German nerves settled back to normal)
from seven in the evening to nine in the morning. After eight
days during which no citizen showed his face on the streets at
night, the German troops having been ordered to shoot curfew
violators on sight, the restriction was lifted again and life began
to settle back into its pre-raid pattern. The Gestapo took over the
telephone central and the police station, and Norwegian citizens
were forbidden to make telephone calls. Otherwise, the population was free to carry on its normal business, subject only to the
same restrictions existing elsewhere in Norway.

Even during the eight days of highest tension the Germans
had maintained a careful façade of correctness in their dealings
with the townspeople. On the 30th December, the bodies of
eleven members of the landing force were laid to rest in the
churchyard at South Vaagso with full military honours, including
a service read by the new German chaplain (whose predecessor
had been killed during the raid) and three volleys from a squad
of riflemen. Although the public at large was barred from the
ceremony, eleven prominent citizens were permitted to attend as
a Norwegian guard of honour for the Allied dead.

On the 3rd January workers clearing the wreckage of the
Ulvesund Hotel unearthed another body beneath a tumbled wall;
it was Martin Linge. He was buried beside his British comrades-
in-arms the following day, along with an English sailor whose
remains had just been discovered by divers trying to salvage a
sunken landing craft.[1]

The twin ''Anklet-Archery'' raids brought forth a series of
new decrees from German headquarters in Oslo. Twenty former

---

[1]The craft struck and set afire by the errant bomb from Flight-Sergeant Smith's
aircraft had been pushed off from the landing-point and drifted away in flames, drawing
some fire from the Germans in the town. It later sank in the fjord.

high court officials and close friends of the exiled royal family were arrested in reprisal for what the German Commissioner in Norway, Josef Terboven, called "the kidnapping of eight members of the *Nasjonal Samling* party by Englishmen in violation of international law". Ola Furuseth, a close associate of Vidkun Quisling, suggested that a special home guard of Quisling sympathizers be created in coastal areas. These men would receive special training and then be detailed to stand guard at critical points along the coast to protect *Nasjonal Samling* officials "who risk being carried off by the British". This plan died stillborn, for lack of volunteers; there just were not enough German sympathizers left in Norway.

The escape of large groups of civilians with the landing forces focused attention on a dangerous trend: on re-examining their records, the Germans discovered that over one hundred former Norwegian officers had escaped to England to carry on the fight. Gestapo squads went out on to the streets and began re-arresting the Air Force and Navy officers who had been paroled after the fall of Norway.

But the decree which had the greatest potential impact on the citizens of South Vaagso had to do with the men who had escaped. Not only were their male relatives to be arrested, but now all chattel property and cattle owned by either the escaper or his parents would be confiscated, and his house burned to the ground. This edict caused considerable soul-searching by the commanders on the scene, and was stoutly resisted by the local *lensmann*,[1] a stubborn islander named Jacob Refvik, who protested violently. Refvik demanded and won an opportunity to present his views before a council of the senior German officers in the town before any action was taken.

His basic argument was that the authorities issuing the order in distant Oslo could not possibly have understood the situation currently existing in South Vaagso. Two hotels and twenty homes had been destroyed in the raid; as a result, some families were already doubled up in available housing. Burning more homes would only aggravate the situation, and burning the homes of all those who left with the raiders would actually put innocent people out on the street. Such an order was not only unjust, it was inhuman.

---

[1] A combination of police officer and civil servant who operates in Norwegian country districts.

Refvik fought out his case before the German area commissioner, four *Nasjonal Samling* officials, and representatives of the office of Reichskommissar Terboven. He played skilfully upon the hopes of each group to maintain a certain image in the eyes of the citizens: the Germans were still determined to be "correct" in their dealings with the citizens of occupied territories; the *Nasjonal Samling* party was still hoping to show that it kept the best interests of the people of Norway foremost in its mind.

In the end, he won his case; the homes were spared. But to a German, orders are sacred, and everyone felt that some ritual burning must take place in order to comply with the letter if not the spirit of the decree. In a peculiar note of comic relief appended to the more tragic events of the raid, the furniture in the selected homes was evacuated to safety and replaced with boxes and barrels of rubbish, which were then dutifully burned. Afterwards a report was prepared certifying that "fires had been set in the homes and all the contents destroyed" and official eyes looked carefully elsewhere while the undamaged furniture was replaced in the rooms. The Germans saw nothing funny in this at all. *"Befehl ist befehl!"* ("An order is an order!") To be truthful, neither did the Norwegians at the time; they were too relieved to see critically needed housing spared the torch.

Henceforth, the Germans became even more truculent and harder to deal with. Violators of even minor regulations met with severe punishment, and the next time Lensmann Refvik raised his voice against authority he was summarily relieved of his job and banished from the town; he had used up his authority, so far as the Germans were concerned, in staving off the disastrous situation that would have developed had the houses been burnt.

But the peculiar events that occurred in the town were only a symptom of the confusion and consternation the raid had generated in Berlin.

25

REACTIONS IN BERLIN

Hitler had been growing nervous about the defences of Norway even before the "Archery-Anklet" blow fell. Alarmed by unconfirmed reports that the Allies, newly strengthened by the recent addition of the United States to the list of active combatants, were contemplating a major operation in Scandinavia, he demanded to know whether a large-scale invasion of Norway could be beaten off.

On Christmas Day, 1941, while the "Archery" force still lay at anchor at Sollum Voe pumping excess water out of the troopships after the violent passage from Scapa Flow and awaiting more favourable weather to proceed with the attack, *O.K.W.*, German Army Headquarters in Berlin, ordered an immediate and prompt re-evaluation of the situation in Norway. Did General von Falkenhorst feel prepared to deal with any major allied adventures in his zone of responsibility?

Falkenhorst concluded that with his present resources he probably would find himself unable to repel an attack in any great force, and his reply included an urgent appeal for 12,000 replacements to bring his combat divisions up to fighting strength; too much precious manpower had been frittered away in manning the myriad of small commands and garrisons which seem to mushroom in occupied territory, and his combat losses from the 1940 campaign had not yet been made good. Furthermore, German defensive power was stretched paper-thin along the length of Norway's tortuous coastline; three additional divisions, said Falkenhorst, would be needed to "beef up" his small reserve and permit him to lay out a defence in greater depth.

The staff at *O.K.W.* were just mulling over this disquieting reply when first word of the Vaagso attack burst like a bombshell on Berlin. The "Anklet" thrust in the Lofotens had come and gone, momentarily distracting German attention from the more southerly areas; some damage had been done, but the prompt displacement of Luftwaffe formations to the danger zone seemed to have forced a hasty British withdrawal. Reconnaissance aircraft were following the withdrawing "Anklet" force and had discovered Admiral Tovey's manoeuvring of the Home Fleet in northern waters, a diversion which succeeded completely in its role of distracting German naval intelligence during the approach of the "Archery" force. Hour-by-hour reports from coastal patrol aircraft gave the latest positions of the major British vessels, whose movements were followed with almost hypnotic fascination at headquarters in Oslo. A German troopship, *Kong Ring,* carrying soldiers bound for home leave in Germany, struck a mine and went down in the North Sea; the Commanding Admiral, Norway, pressed all available resources into the conduct of rescue operations.

And then under cover of all these distractions Admiral Burrough slipped the "Archery" force undetected into Vaagsfjord and Number 3 Commando exploded into the surprised German garrison. The Combined Chiefs of Staff could hardly have picked a more opportune moment to unleash operation "Archery".

There is an old military adage to the effect that one of the most lucrative objectives for a military commander is the mind of the enemy commander. Unknowingly, the British had scored a direct hit on this target without really aiming at it. One of the original aims of the operation had been stated as "harassment" of the German coastal defences, but no one in London could possibly have foreseen the ensuing panic in Berlin. It only goes to prove what far-reaching effects a minimum of force may have if applied at the exact optimum moment.

No one at *O.K.W.* had any doubts about how the Fuehrer would react to the news of this British sortie, and the initial report of some sort of an allied landing at Vaagso drew a request for further details by the quickest available means. The second report out of Oslo was hardly more satisfactory; the landing force had withdrawn, and it was impossible to assess the exact intent of the operation after the fact. Details of the action were obscure in many particulars, and no prisoners had been taken. The precise aim was questionable: had the British merely intended to make the coastal defences jumpy, a logical enough mission in the continual war of nerves being waged in occupied territories? Or had this perhaps been a reconnaissance in force with an eye to future—and significantly larger—landings?

The Fuehrer demanded that his military chiefs tell him what the landing meant and *O.K.W.* drew up a hasty study, which suggested that the purpose of the quick one-two thrust in Norway could very well have been to probe for soft spots in the coastal defences. The landing in the Lofotens, the second in the same spot, had been no great military feat since the northern-most portion of the country was lightly defended; but the confidence and daring with which the southern force had lanced into a heavily-protected area was a possible indication of growing boldness, and a readiness on the part of the Allies to hurl their forces into the teeth of a prepared defence. The British might even be toying with the idea of landing larger forces on the Norwegian coast to secure permanent bases from which to menace German shipping in coastal waters and—if successful— bring all such shipping to a standstill.

This report lay on Hitler's desk on the 29th December when his military staff filed into the room for a conference which was to have a decisive effect upon the course of the war.

Admiral Raeder, the Chief of Naval Staff, gave a preliminary report of the actions in Norway on the 26th and 27th, and Generalfeldmarschall Keitel, the Fuehrer's chief of staff, briefly outlined the content of the *O.K.W.* estimate for the benefit of those who had not yet seen it. Then Hitler began to speak about the ramifications of the British action. The raid had crystallized his misgivings about the state of affairs in Norway.

"If the British go about things properly," he said, "they will attack northern Norway at several points. By means of an all-out attack by their fleet and ground troops they will try to displace us there, take Narvik if possible, and thus exert pressure on Sweden and Finland. This might be of decisive importance for the outcome of the war.

"The German fleet must therefore use all its forces for the defence of Norway. It would be expedient to transfer all battle-ships and pocket-battleships there for this purpose."

One did not ordinarily argue with the Fuehrer, but this declaration threw the naval chiefs into consternation. Admiral Raeder hastened to point out that the battleships *Scharnhorst* and *Gneisenau* were at the moment bottled up in the French port of Brest, along with the heavy cruiser *Prinz Eugen*. The only short route into Norwegian waters lay through the English Channel, firmly blockaded by the Royal Navy. The alternative would be to go all the way around the British Isles, far beyond supporting range of the Luftwaffe for most of the trip but always within striking range of the R.A.F., who could be expected to react vigorously. Surely the Fuehrer would not think of forcing the Brest group to run the British blockade?

But that was precisely what the Fuehrer was thinking of doing, and he would not be swayed by cries of "impossible" from his admirals. There must be some way of breaking through the Channel blockade, and the admirals must find it; the battleships were urgently required in Norway. On this note the meeting ended.

During the next few weeks Hitler's apprehensions about Norway continued to grow, while the admirals dragged their feet, hoping that his ardour would cool and he would reconsider his decision to mass the German fleet in Norwegian waters. It came to a showdown in mid-January of 1942, when the Fuehrer sent for Raeder and informed him that recent intelligence reports gave positive indication that Britain and the United States were indeed planning large-scale landings in Norway. Sweden could be expected to co-operate with the Allies in return for Narvik and the rich ore deposits at Petsamo, and with an allied lodgement secured in Scandinavia Germany would gradually be squeezed out of the Baltic. Attempts might be made within the next few weeks to secure footholds along the coast between Trondheim and Kirkenes; a major offensive would follow in the spring.

"Norway," he pronounced, "is the zone of destiny in this war. I demand unconditional obedience to my commands and directives concerning the defence of this area."

While the unhappy Grand Admiral fidgeted uncomfortably, Hitler went on to outline what he expected of the armed forces. The navy must take all necessary measures to cripple the allied offensive at its inception. *All* warships, not just the battleships and heavy cruisers, must be deployed forthwith; even E–boats and submarines would find a vital role in the coming operations. The Brest group must somehow break through the Channel and join the rest of Germany's capital ships. No other operations would be given a higher priority, except for elements engaged in the Mediterranean theatre of operations.

Raeder took his courage in his hands and tried one last time to dissuade the Fuehrer from imposing what he still considered an unconscionable risk on the battleships of the Brest group, but in the end all he accomplished was to get the submarine fleet exempted from the move to Norway on the basis that their

E-Boat

presence in the western Atlantic was critical for Germany's future; the battle of the convoys was raging at its height.

Advised of the Fuehrer's conclusion that events in Norway would shape the future of the war, *O.K.W.* hastened to reinforce Falkenhorst. The 12,000 replacements he had requested were made available immediately, plus 18,000 more organized into "fortress" battalions. Another armoured division was activated in Norway to back up these elements and stiffen the defence. Shipments of up-to-date coast defence guns and stocks of ammunition were given high priority, and the old relics with which the Germans had faced the "Archery" force were consigned to the scrap heap. New networks of field fortifications sprang up at critical points along the coast.

It is difficult to surmise just what information led Hitler to conclude that the Allies were in fact preparing to move against Norway in force. To be sure, Operation "Jupiter", a plan to land in Norway and "unroll the map of Europe from the north", had once been a pet idea of Winston Churchill's, but the Prime Minister never succeeded in selling the scheme to his chiefs of staff, who were aware of the nightmarish logistical implications, and it died in council. Preliminary deliberations on this plan had been conducted in greatest secrecy, and it is unlikely that Hitler could have been aware of them. More likely he had put himself in Churchill's place, devised a similar plan out of his own fertile imagination, and then watched anxiously for signs that it was actually in motion. That the little pinprick thrusts in December served to feed this paranoia was in the end their most fruitful result.

In February Hitler sent Generalfeldmarschall List, Armed Forces Commander South-East, as his personal representative to make an inspection tour of the Scandinavian area and determine whether the additional measures thus far taken were adequate to ensure the defence of Norway. On List's recommendation three new divisional commands were established, even more coast artillery weapons were shipped to Norway, and additional defensive installations went up not only along the coast but in the interior of the country as well.

The reinforcement of Norway was by now progressing like a gigantic chain reaction, and each minor incident of sabotage by the underground and each allied aircraft flying over Norwegian territory was taken as additional confirmation of a vast design, further increasing the invasion hysteria. By 6th June, 1944, the day the Allies landed in Normandy, 372,000 German troops were sitting idly by in Norway, guarding against an invasion that never came and was in fact never seriously contemplated. It is interesting to speculate what effect even a third of those 372,000 men might have had upon the outcome of the campaign in Normandy, or on the Russian front where the situation had grown equally critical.

Meanwhile, the capital ships of the German fleet gathered in Norwegian waters. First to arrive was the battleship *Tirpitz*, which slipped in safely from the Baltic and went into hiding deep in a northern fjord, her decks and rigging miraculously blossoming forth with fir trees. Then, on 11th February, 1942, the Brest group made their move.

Late that night, under cover of foul weather, *Scharnhorst*, *Gneisenau* and *Prinz Eugen* slipped out of Brest and plunged northward into the Channel. British radar picked them up the next morning as they approached the Strait of Dover, and British

ircraft roared in through the murk to drop mines in their path
nd lay torpedoes against their hulls at point-blank range. The
ierman warships laid down a withering barrage of anti-aircraft
ire, shooting down English planes right and left, but in the end
iey were all hit, *Gneisenau* suffering such severe damages that
he had to put into Kiel for repairs. British bombers found her
iere later in the month and holed her again, but a battleship is a
ard target to kill and eventually she got through to Norway.
charnhorst too sustained heavy damages in the Channel dash,
ut won free in the end and limped into her new fjord home the
ollowing day. *Prinz Eugen* made it to Trondheim, but a torpedo
ad blown off her rudder and she subsequently returned to
iermany for repairs.[1]

If this successful breakout through what the British had
lways been pleased to consider a local pond created a scandal in
ie halls of the Admiralty, its end result, the concentration of
iost of the German fleet in Norwegian waters, delighted the
oyal Navy. In March and April, *Hipper* and *Luetzow* joined
ieir sisters in Norway and the British found that by putting the
ork in the bottle they could contain one battleship, three heavy
ruisers, eight destroyers, four E–boats and twenty submarines in
rctic waters with only a minimal force of their own. True, these
ierman fleet elements posed a mortal threat to convoys making
ie perilous northern run to Russia, but it was a far simpler thing
o provide strong escorts to these convoys than to cover the
vhole north Atlantic convoy route against commerce raiders.
he true importance of Adolf Hitler's fateful decision to concen-
rate his naval resources is underlined by the fact that none of
iese ships ever again got loose in the Atlantic. Eventually all
vere either destroyed in battle along the Arctic convoy route or
racked down by the R.A.F. to their hiding places in the northern
iords and bombed out of the war.

And in the long run, the successful breakout through the
Channel, precipitated by the twin "Archery-Anklet" thrusts in
Norway, had still one more significant and far-reaching effect on
ie course of the war. Hitler, who had risked three of his capital
hips against the best advice of his professional naval staff, saw
is own judgement vindicated; he was right and they were
vrong. From this time onward he never hesitated to overrule his

Scharnhorst

military advisers when facing critical decisions, especially when
they preached caution, and the history of the later years of the
war is a catalogue of fatal mistakes dictated by a megalomaniac
in Berlin who ignored the professional counsel of the skilled and
competent commanders of his armed forces.

26

LESSONS OF VAAGSO

Beyond its unexpected strategic ramifications, the relatively
small-scale attack at Vaagso was yet to bear fruit in an entirely
different field. For in evaluating the tactical lessons learned
during the operation, the planners responsible for joint operations
and amphibious warfare uncovered some new principles, plus a
few dramatic reiterations of old ones.

First and foremost was confirmation that joint planning and
joint preparation could pay real dividends in joint operations. It
may be argued that this point is so obvious as to be apparent to
even the dullest military thinker, but surprisingly enough the
Vaagso raid gives military history its first example of a truly
tri-service operation, planned and developed from its very inception by representatives of the three services functioning as a joint
team, each member working to perfect his own service's allotted
portion of the over-all plan in close co-ordination with his
counterparts from the other services. Indeed the only notable
failure in the operation, the R.A.F.'s deck-to-air radio link the
default of which accounted for the needless loss of several
British aircraft, sprang from the one serious breach in the
otherwise high standard of tri-service co-operation in planning
and preparation—the R.A.F. communicators had been so confident of their system that they had disdained to practise it during
the rehearsal exercises.

The Royal Navy learned a lot about the operation of
boarding parties, handling of armed trawlers encountered during
operations, and the peculiar requirements of operating in such
restricted waters; the Special Service Brigade developed some

new ideas for preparing its Commandos for street fighting, and the R.A.F. had not only learned the hard way about the problems of air-to-surface communications, but had also gained useful experience in the conduct of long-range aerial support which would prove invaluable later in the war. To the student of military history the Vaagso raid stands as an example of that most desirable but unusual achievement: the carefully-prepared military operation which comes off almost exactly as planned, running smoothly along its preordained course with each developing contingency foreseen and provided for. In the end, the real strength of the Vaagso plan of operation lay not in its rigidity but in its flexibility, allowing maximum leeway to commanders who could think on their feet by providing them with a variety of means to achieve each desired end, risks and possible enemy reactions realistically considered, and plans, alternate plans and options developed accordingly. At each level, commanders had been given their missions in broad terms and were left to work out the details for themselves.

No one had expected the landing force to come away without casualties, but in practice the casualties had been lighter than anticipated, especially diring the initial landings. After the Maaloy battery had been overrun it developed that the battle was just beginning, for German resistance in the town itself proved unexpectedly stiff; the defenders of Sebelin's improvised second line did their work with surprising skill and determination for a patchwork force, but the flexibility of the ground plan allowed Haydon and Durnford-Slater a sufficient variety of options—especially where employment of the reserve force was concerned—to enable them to readjust to the situation even more effectively than did the Germans. The naval force had taken a significant toll of enemy shipping in executing a similarly flexible plan of operation under the guidance of an intelligent and quick-witted commander who always had sufficient information—painstakingly culled for him in London before the plan was developed—to weigh the contrasting benefits and risks of each course of action before deciding how to meet any new situation. The requisite facts were at his fingertips when the moment called for instant decisions.

The idea of keeping the uncommitted reserves afloat until needed so as to facilitate rapid deployment to any critical area was itself a brilliant innovation of the planners back at Richmond Terrace. This too may seem obvious to the trained amphibious

warfare specialist of today, who had the concept drummed into
his head during a succession of staff courses, but it was in
December 1941 that the concept originated in a pleasant little
Whitehall room looking out over the Thames, where a small
group of planners racked their brains for solutions to the immediate tactical problems of a projected assault on the German garrison at Vaagso. From the same fertile minds sprang the idea of
staging a diversionary air attack timed to draw the defenders'
attention skyward during the final critical minutes as the landing
force closed on its assigned beaches.

All these new concepts would be reflected again and again
in the course of the war, sometimes exactly as developed at
Vaagso and sometimes in even more refined form. From Number
2 Commando's daring sally into the St. Nazaire docks a few
months later, to the beaches of Dieppe in less than a year; along
the coasts of North Africa, Sicily, Italy and Normandy; throughout the long chain of island-hopping amphibious assaults in the
Pacific; wherever major landings were contemplated in future
operations of the war, the final plans could trace parts of their
lineage back to the Vaagso raid, a tiny parent which spawned a
legion of huge and powerful children.

Brigadier Haydon, reflecting later upon the significant "firsts"
scored at Vaagso, was inclined to shrug them off: "It struck none
of us at the time that we were breaking new ground, or devising
a new technique. It all seemed perfectly reasonable and good
common sense."

During the summer of 1942 Haydon's ex-brigade major,
Robert Henriques, Commander de Costabadie, and Group-Captain
Homer of the R.A.F. were chosen to go to the United States to
assist in the planning of Operation "Torch", the allied invasion
of North Africa. They tried to convince their American counterparts of the value of close interservice co-operation in preparing
the assault, but the staggering political and logistical implications
of the operation so hypnotized the U.S. planners that they paid
little attention to the relatively low-ranking British advisers
propounding what seemed a radically new concept of staff
procedure; there were already sufficient problems to deal with
without rewriting existing field manuals.

The assault got ashore successfully in November but there
were so many snags and kinks in interservice co-ordination—
some of them major and costly and some of them minor and
insignificant but almost all of them avoidable—that when Gener-

al Patton was assigned to begin planning for the invasion of
Sicily he sent Mountbatten an urgent request from North Africa:
might he borrow some officers experienced in joint planning,
including Henriques? The request was of course approved and
Colonel Henriques recorded the result:

> It was in a cork forest in North Africa...and
> subsequently in the Naval Headquarters at Bizerta
> where we achieved a degree of integrated planning
> which exceeded that of Vaagso....
>
> Admiral [Connolly] and General Truscott were so
> convinced of the value of this specialized integrated
> planning that they went so far as to make each naval
> officer share his bedroom with his military counterpart,
> and to insist that at mealtimes, at the table where the
> admiral presided, naval and military officers should sit
> alternatively. It paid very handsome dividends on the
> beaches.

Epilogue

Vaagso today shows few signs that it was ever the scene of a
major combat action. Most of the scars are gone, and the
destroyed and damaged buildings have long since been rebuilt.
Meanwhile, the burgeoning population of prosperous modern
Norway has created a marked expansion in even obscure fishing
villages.

New homes stand on the former site of the German strongpoint facing the strait, and the visitor who walks out along the
new causeway connecting Seternes Point with Maaloy Island will
find another large structure situated just where the German
battery once had its barracks; nearby, only a few shallow depres-
sions in the ground mark the points where the guns were once
located.

Tourists come and go again during the summer months, just

as they did before the war. There are not many of them, as the cruise ships tend to bypass this obscure point in their trips through the better-known scenic fjords, and it is unlikely that many ever learn or even suspect the part that this peaceful village once played in the violent events of the war. As everywhere else in Norway, the citizens prefer not to talk of those unpleasant days; the subjects of conversation are more apt to be the traditional ones: canning-factory gossip, the new engine Peer is installing in his trawler, taxes, and where the fish are running this week.

And what of the men who sailed into Vaagsfjord that cold December morning?

Brigadier Haydon and Admiral Burrough quickly went on to bigger things. Haydon moved up after the raid to become deputy to Admiral Mountbatten at Combined Operations Headquarters and one of the British Army's acknowledged authorities on joint operations. He retired at war's end as a major-general. Admiral Burrough won further distinction and promotion, and before he retired a full admiral in 1946 with a knighthood and an impressive list of British and foreign decorations and awards he served a tour of post-war duty as British Naval Commander-in-Chief, Germany. Captain Denny also rose to the top of his profession, retiring in the same rank as his former commander, and with a comparable list of honours.

After Vaagso, Number 3 Commando went on to blaze a trail across the continent of Europe, taking part in the great raid at Dieppe, then moving to the Mediterranean to spearhead the allied landings in Sicily and Italy. The unit then returned to England for the cross-channel assault into Normandy and the long drive across France, Holland, Belgium, and Germany. By the end of the war it had become one of the foremost small units in the history of the British Army, its members having won during its brief five-year history eight admissions to the Distinguished Service Order, more than thirty Military Crosses, a similar number of Military Medals and five Distinguished Conduct Medals. Too few of the Vaagso veterans who helped win those decorations were around to celebrate by then: Doctor Corry fell at Dieppe, Captain Ronald (temporarily detached from the Commando) in the landings at Algiers, Lieutenant Lloyd and Trooper Croft in Sicily, Lieutenant Pooley and Lance-Sergeant Herbert (by then a lieutenant himself) in Normandy.

Later actions of the war took their toll of Number 2

Commando's Vaagso veterans, too, especially the heroic assault at St. Nazaire; Captains Birney and Hooper went there with most of their men. Hooper, seriously wounded, was one of the lucky few who returned, while Birney died in action. Most of the surviving members of their troops wound up in German prison camps, where before many months they were joined by old comrades from Vaagso days; Lieutenant Clement, Lance-Sergeant Connolly, Troopers Halls, Clark, Sherington, Hilton and several others fell into German hands at Dieppe. Soon afterwards, Lieutenant Graeme Black, who won his M.C. with Hooper at Vaagso, was taken prisoner during the ill-fated Glomfjord operation and summarily shot by his German captors.

Durnford-Slater soon moved up to brigade command and Peter Young, wearing a D.S.O. from Dieppe, took over Number 3 Commando; when Young in turn went on to higher rank and greater responsibilities, Arthur Komrower, newly recovered from his Vaagso injuries, succeeded him in command and saw the unit through the rest of the war.

When Number 2 Commando's gallant commanding officer, Lieutenant-Colonel A. C. Newman, V.C., was taken prisoner at St. Nazaire, Jack Churchill transferred over from Number 3 to reorganize and refit the unit, and led Number 2 with flair and distinction, winning himself two D.S.O.s before the unhappy morning when he too fell into enemy hands. But Churchill's war was far from over; shipped to a concentration camp in Germany instead of to the usual prisoner-of-war compound, he tunnelled out in company with four other British prisoners but was recaptured after fifteen days on the run. He was then sent to a smaller camp near Innsbruck, from which he escaped through the Brenner Pass into Italy, successfully reaching the lines of the advancing 88th U.S. Infantry Division.

Lieutenant O'Flaherty rejoined the commandos after two years in hospital and eight major operations, minus an eye but still full of fight. He survived the war and in the early 1950 action again with the British Commonwealth Brigade in Korea, where he was decorated by the American Army for gallantry in action. As this is written he is still on active duty.

Durnford-Slater left the army after the war, serving for a short time as burser at Bedford School before accepting a position as personnel manager for a large London precision instruments firm. Peter Young chose to remain on active duty. He reverted to his permanent rank and subsequently commanded the

9th Regiment of the Arab Legion in Jordan for several years. In 1959 he retired from active duty to become head of the Military History Department at the Royal Military Academy, Sandhurst.

In 1950 Colonel Churchill, Lieutenant-Colonel Komrower and Captain O'Flaherty were invited to visit Vaagso with a group of officers from the Royal Marine Commandos, who in the course of their schooling had been required to work out a plan for a raid based on the situation pertaining in 1941 and were now going to walk over the ground and see how their plan might actually have worked in practice. As they strolled through the town, O'Flaherty met the baker's wife, whom he had last seen crawling through the window of her blazing home nearly nine years earlier. She recognized him at once and ran to get her husband, and the three soon were sitting down to coffee together in the baker's rebuilt home, chatting like old friends.

The spirit that carried those young men of England and Norway to Vaagso has not been lost with the passing of years, and those who fell were not quickly forgotten. On 15th June, 1943, as Number 3 Commando made its final preparations for the assault on Sicily, Durnford-Slater told the assembled officers: "You officers have got to set the pace once we get ashore. It isn't enough to tell your men 'Nip along there, I'll be along in a minute'—the operational stage is where you really earn your pay. Remember Vaagso. Algy Forrester was the man who really won that one for us, by going like hell down the main street."

More than twenty years after the raid a former member of 3 Troop reminisced about Captain Giles, recounting incidents that typified the manner in which Giles inspired every man of the troop to give everything he had to the task at hand. He concluded his account this way: "I remember my old captain very well and, whenever I can, in November I place a small cross in the Commando Field of Remembrance at Westminster Abbey for him. He had high standards and was a first-class officer and gentleman. I would have followed him anywhere and, thank goodness, I eventually shall."

But the last word belongs to Denis O'Flaherty: "When I rejoined at the end of 1943 the Commandos had gone on to the 'me and my pal' system. No one moved without cover from his mate. Fire and movement were second nature—whether this stemmed from Vaagso I don't know. Certainly a close look at street fighting and fire support resulted from Vaagso. We in Number 3 Commando were conscious of our paucity of communications and that was why I was on a signals course prior to the raid.

"One thing that is quite clear to me is that 1 Commando Brigade, by 1944, was a very fine professional set-up, with command, control and tactical know-how far ahead of ordinary infantry, and far advanced from the good old days of 1941.

"At the same time, and quite rightly, they had lost the blind dash that I thought was remarkable in the minority who were actually engaged at close quarters at Vaagso. I have never seen that equalled in any army since."

Appendix 1

OFFICIAL COMMUNIQUES
28th December, 1941

LONDON—On Saturday, 27th December, a small-scale raid, mainly against enemy shipping, was carried out on the Norwegian coast by the combined force of the Royal Navy, Army, and R.A.F.

The operation was entirely successful in all respects and all of our ships returned fit for immediate service.

A further communiqué will be issued as soon as details are available.

BERLIN—British naval forces on 27th December attempted a surprise attack at two remote points of the Norwegian coast. After brief violent engagements the British landing detachments were ejected by local patrols of the Army and Navy. The British landing detachments retired to their ships.

German bombers sank a destroyer of the fleeing warship formation. A cruiser and another destroyer were damaged. Ten enemy bombers were shot down in air fights and by our anti-aircraft artillery.

During the approach of the enemy the German patrol boat *Föhn* was attacked by numerous bombers. The patrol boat shot down one enemy bomber and then lost in heroic struggle against the superior fire of a British cruiser and several destroyers. Some

Norwegian merchant ships which were engaged in peaceful coast traffic were attacked and sunk by the British.

Appendix 2

AWARDS AND DECORATIONS FOR OPERATION "ARCHERY"
Announced in the London Gazette, *3rd April, 1942*

Bar to D.S.O.
  Brigadier J. C. Haydon, D.S.O., O.B.E.
D.S.O.
  Rear-Admiral H. M. Burrough, C.B.
  Lieutenant-Colonel J. F. Durnford-Slater, R.A., Number 3 Commando
  Wing-Commander J.F.G. Jenkins, D.F.C.
  Lieutenant D. W. V. P. O'Flaherty, R.A., Number 3 Commando
  Wing-Commander R. J. Oxley, D.F.C.
  Group-Captain A. H. Willetts
D.S.C.
  Lieutenant P. N. Bowman, R.N.V.R.
  Lieutenant N. P. C. Hastings, R.N.V.R.
  Sub-Lieutenant P.A.R. Hayes, R.N.
  Sub-Lieutenant M. P. Vaux, R.N.
M.C.
  Lieutenant G. D. Black, South Lancashire Regiment, Number 2 Commando
  Captain P. Young, Bedfordshire and Hertfordshire Regiment, Number 3 Commando

Bar to D.F.C.
   Flying Officer H. P. Brancker, D.F.C.
D.S.M.
   Leading Seaman L. Chaisty
   Leading Seaman A. E. Clixby-Watson
   Leading Stoker J. Goff
   Chief Stoker J. Graham
   Petty Officer Cook W. Kefford
D.C.M.
   Lance-Sergeant R. G. Herbert, M.M., Northamptonshire
      Regiment, Number 3 Commando
   Corporal E. G. White, Q.O. Royal West Kent Regiment,
      Number 3 Commando
M.M.
   Corporal M. B. Fitzpatrick, Royal Tank Regiment, R.A.C.

Mention in Despatches
   Lance-Sergeant J. D. Allen, Royal Armoured Corps, Num-
      ber 3 Commando
   Lieutenant-Commander L. W. L. Argles, R.N.
   Lientenant N. A. Bacon, R.N.V.R.
   Captain E. W. Bradley, Inniskilling Fusiliers, Number 3 Com-
      mando
   Petty Officer C. E. Brookes
   Lieutenant-Commander W. S. Byles, R. D., R.N.R.
   Lieutenant R. W. H. Chancellor, R.N.V.R.
   Leading Sick Berth Attendant E. T. Clough
   Captain S. D. Corry, M.B., R.A.M.C., Number 3 Commando
   Lieutenant-Commander A. N. P. de Costabadie, D.S.C., R.N.
   Leading Seaman W. H. Courage
   Lieutenant W. W. Etches, Royal Warwickshire Regiment,
      Number 3 Commando
   Commander W. R. Fell, O.B.E., D.S.C., R.N. (ret.)
   Corporal G. A. Fyson, Royal Berkshire Regiment, Number 3
      Commando
   Chief Petty Officer G. Hopkins
   Able Seaman F. W. Joyce
   Lieutenant A. H. Laight, R.N.V.R.
   Lieutenant-Commander (E) J. Law, R.N.R.
   Lieutenant D. W. V. P. O'Flaherty, R.A., Number 3 Commando

Sergeant G. Ramsay, R.A., Number 3 Commando
Leading Seaman L. Robinson
Fusilier D. H. Roderick, Royal Scots Fusiliers, Number 3
  Commando
Surgeon-Lieutenant J. P. G. Rogerson, M.B.,C.H.B., R.N.V.R.
Stoker First Class W. Stevenson
Private T. Verner, Argyle and Sutherland Highlanders, Num-
  ber 3 Commando
Petty Officer E. B. Ward
Lieutenant-Commander M. E. Wevell, R.N.
Able Seaman E. Willcox
Leading Seaman J. Williams
Able Seaman D.C.H. Wood

INDEX

ABOUT THE AUTHOR

JOSEPH H. DEVINS, JR. was raised in Michigan and graduated from West Point in 1952. Much of his early service was with the Army Special Forces and other airborne units and he later served on the faculty of the US Army Command and General Staff College. A veteran of service in Europe, Latin America and the Far East including two tours of duty in Vietnam, he retired from active duty in 1975 and now lives in Colorado, where he and his wife are surrounded by a large and constantly-varying assortment of children, grandchildren and animals.

While on active duty he was an occasional contributor to military journals. About the origins of this book he writes: "I was doing some research on combined operations when I happened to read that one small Commando raid at Vaagso had strategic consequences out of all proportion to the forces employed. This sounded like the makings of an interesting article. Subsequent correspondence with veterans of the raiding force—some of the most wonderful men in the world—and with agencies holding records of the operation unearthed so much fascinating material that the project soon snowballed into a book. The research was a lot of fun. Being done entirely by mail, it took about four years of my spare time and resembled doing a jigsaw puzzle by remote control."

THE MASTERFUL NEW SUPERTHRILLER BY
THE BESTSELLING AUTHOR OF FIREFOX

Craig Thomas

JADE TIGER

Out of the sea and into the hands of British SIS
agents, Hyde and Aubrey, comes a Chinese defector
with earth-shattering news: Wolfgang Zimmermann—
respected architect of the treaty that will tear down
the Berlin Wall—is really a Russian spy. In a murder-
ous race against time, Hyde and Aubrey clash with
CIA, KGB, and Chinese espionage agents in an explosive international struggle for power.

Buy JADE TIGER on sale July 15, 1983, wherever
Bantam paperbacks are sold, or use this handy cou-
pon for ordering: